"As the economy enter ners and losers. The strength of niche companies lies in their ability to adapt quickly to changing times and find opportunities to succeed where larger companies might fail. *Battling Big Box* provides a road map for entrepreneurs looking to strengthen their management skills in order to build successful and flexible niche companies. The book is not just a theoretical piece on how to succeed. Rather, a number of actual cases are covered describing how the entrepreneurs have met the challenges and overcame them on the road to success. It covers a variety of industries with varying strategies. The lessons learned from this book are not limited to small businesses. Every business should benefit from the contents of this book."

—Sung Won Sohn, economist, businessman, and professor of economics and finance at California State University

"Industries—the media industry especially—are undergoing unprecedented change and niche companies are emerging as winners in a number of areas. *Battling Big Box* can be an essential tool to help talented people learn entrepreneurial skills and create their own successful companies."

—Sree Sreenivasan, professor, dean of student affairs and director of the New Media program, Columbia Graduate School of Journalism

"Small business is the backbone of the U.S. economy. It provides more than half of the nation's jobs and most of its job growth. Marks and Dubroff use information gleaned from dozens of interviews with successful small business owners, as well as their own business experience, to provide a succinct how-to guide for small businesses that want to grow and succeed."

—Tucker Hart Adams, economist and president of The Adams Group, Inc.

"With so many small businesses failing every day, you might think it is impossible to beat the Big Box stores like Wal-Mart, Best Buy, and Home Depot at their own games. But you'd be wrong. Noted journalists Marks and Dubroff, in *Battling Big Box*, explain exactly how small businesses are adapting and holding onto their customers and market share despite the Big Box onslaught. The book is filled with fascinating interviews from small businesspeople who have succeeded, and it is also filled with valuable resources to arm you in your battle with the Bigs."

—Jordan E. Goodman, "America's Money Answers Man," and author of *Fast Profits in Hard Times*

"Succeeding in a small business requires an ability to think strategically while dealing with day-to-day tactical issues and challenges. This book not only shows you how, it succeeds in practicing what it preaches. It will show you how to assess the big picture without missing the little things."

—Alan J. Parisse, sales expert, and author of *Questions Great Advisors Ask and Investors Need to Know*

BATTLING BIG BOX

HOW NIMBLE NICHE COMPANIES CAN OUTMANEUVER GIANT COMPETITORS

By Henry Dubroff and
Susan J. Marks

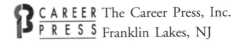

CAREER PRESS The Career Press, Inc.
Franklin Lakes, NJ

BATTLING BIG BOX
EDITED AND TYPESET BY GINA TALUCCI
Cover design by The Design Works Group
Printed in the U.S.A. by Book-mart Press

To order this title, please call toll-free 1-800-CAREER-1 (NJ and Canada: 201-848-0310) to order using VISA or MasterCard, or for further information on books from Career Press.

The Career Press, Inc., 3 Tice Road, PO Box 687,
Franklin Lakes, NJ 07417
www.careerpress.com

Library of Congress Cataloging-in-Publication Data

Dubroff, Henry.
    Battling big box : how nimble niche companies can outmaneuver giant competitors / by Henry Dubroff and Susan J. Marks.
        p. cm.
    Includes bibliographical references and index.
    ISBN 978-1-60163-028-5
        1. Small business—Management. 2. Market segmentation—Management. 3. New business enterprises—Management. I. Marks, Susan J. II. Title. III. Title: Niche companies can outmaneuver giant competitors.

HD62.7.D835 2009
658.02'2--dc22

2008041376

DEDICATION

To Gilda and Sol, the best parents a son could imagine, and to Ona for putting up with the worst of all possible situations—a spouse who starts a small business, then writes a book about it.

—Henry

To Ethel and Henry, thank you. And to John and Emma for their unwavering support and tolerance.

—Susan

ACKNOWLEDGMENTS

This book would not have been possible without the insight, vision, help, and teachings of the many people who have shared their wisdom and skills with us throughout the years. To all these people, we thank you.

Thank you, too, to the individuals, entrepreneurs, experts, and businessmen and women who willingly and openly shared their stories for this book. We hope your lessons learned and wisdom shared will help others fulfill their entrepreneurial dreams of long-term success.

Additionally, we would like to thank the following people:

- The *Pacific Coast Business Times* team for providing endless stories and lessons about business and life, especially Publisher George Wolverton and Vice Chairman John Huggins for countless hours of help and encouragement.

- Carroll Pruett and Jim Lokey for putting me on the program at the annual Mid-State Bank & Trust Economic Symposium where I thought of many of the ideas about small-business success.

- Cynthia Zigmund, our Chicago-based book agent from Literary Services Inc., with her superb vision, perseverance, and unique understanding of the publishing business.
- Kris McGovern, our tireless and wise copyeditor, confidant, and so much more, who is always there no matter what.
- Special thanks to every one of those unsung public relations and marketing heroes who, day in and day out, readily and willingly work tirelessly to provide us with the people and information we need to do our jobs.
- Jordan Goodman, author, speaker, and friend, who started me in this book-writing business.

CONTENTS

INTRODUCTION

Turning any small business into a success is tough. Doing so in a market crowded with Walmart-sized competitors is especially challenging. Yet America's 26 million small-business owners—6 million of them with payrolls to meet—take on the task every year. Thousands fail, but many of those can be attributed to small businesses failing to capitalize on their biggest advantages: size and agility. Their owners/operators fail to recognize that to sustain and grow profits throughout the up-and-down economies requires a multitasking approach that constantly adapts to market changes. Small companies today must adapt if they are going to compete—and beat—the Big Box and chain competition.

The corner grocer, neighborhood hardware store, local manufacturer, or single-location service provider can learn to compete
and prosper against the giants. Acme Hardware in the corner shopping center thrives and grows alongside the mega Home Depot.
Tito's Cuisine down the street fills its tables daily in the shadow of
the local Chili's outlet. Imperial Headwear handles the heat from
giant overseas competition, and Internet-based e-tailer eBags stacks
up big bucks against its worldwide retail competition.

How can that be? Bigger always buries the little competition—
or does it? Size *is* an advantage in the business world. But bigger
isn't necessarily better. These small businesses, and nearly 6 million like them, have found a niche and learned to capitalize on it
in a way that can create a sustainable enterprise. Their small size
means agility and adaptability, customer service and credibility,
that the oversized competition can't begin to match to compete in
a target market.

Battling Big Box ranges far beyond retail and the corner store.
It gives small businesses in every industry the tools necessary to
find the right market and succeed. It offers firsthand lessons from
experts and successful entrepreneurs who share their stories and
teach the lessons you need to win now and over the long haul.

This is a no-nonsense, easily applied guide to the key ingredients essential to building a successful niche company, developing
your own strategic team, and keeping that team energized so you
can win in the shadow of mega-sized competitors. Those key ingredients include:

- **Employee empowerment/the human element:** You'll
  learn how to operate a lean organization with the
  help of technology, trust, and intensity, and to create a dynamic environment in which employees can
  do their best.

- **Effective branding:** We offer an insider's guide to
  what it takes for a niche company to build national,
  regional, and local name recognition right under the
  noses of their Big Box competition.

- **Sales and customers:** Sales are the oxygen supply for your business. Without them, and without your customers, you can't survive.

- **Getting a grip on cash/financial management:** You'll get the inside track on how successful niche companies quickly learn how to track their cash—from following seasonal patterns to raising capital carefully, and separating assets from liabilities. Getting a grip on cash flow is the first step toward effective financial management.

- **Relentless innovation:** We reveal what fuels the relentless innovation that is a part of successful small companies today.

Battling Big Box explains each ingredient in success, how to balance those ingredients, and what it takes to make them work in sync with the other parts of an operation and why, and then explains how to cope with the pitfalls and potholes that threaten to detour an owner/operator from his or her goals. We're not selling overnight success, a program for a price, or a methodology. Instead, this is must-have business advice and quick insight into the everyday problems and solutions that small-business owners face running any company and succeeding against mammoth competition. They're lessons learned firsthand by coauthor Henry Dubroff, a leading financial journalist and owner/operator of a Southern California start-up publishing business in the shadow of competition from the *Los Angeles Times* metropolitan area.

Coauthors Dubroff and Susan J. Marks take you inside the minds of other successful entrepreneurs and business notables who faced their own Goliaths and won. You'll learn firsthand from Joyce Meskis how employee empowerment helps her independent bookstore, The Tattered Cover, compete against Barnes and Noble, Borders, Amazon.com, and more. Jim Wolfe, former CEO of Balance Bar, will share some of the branding and marketing expertise that helped turn a struggling nutrition bar company into a powerhouse.

And advertising executive Cathey M. Finlon, who learned early on
to follow the money, will tell us how to get a grip on cash flow and
how, without it, you can't hope to compete long term against the
giants.

Others who share their lessons learned in *Battling Big Box*
include:

■ Paul Orfalea: This motivational genius began with
one tiny Kinko's office supply and printing store in
1970 and created a world-class business services
empire.

■ J.D. "Jamey" Power: Senior vice president, strategic
advisor, and son of J.D. (Dave) Power, the California
entrepreneur who founded his namesake company,
grew up in the business, and continues the legacy of
promoting excellence and quality in products today.

■ Craig Newmark: This self-declared computer-
programming nerd turned an idea and hobby, his
namesake craigslist.com, into *the* online sensation and forever changed the playing field for classified advertising.

■ Harvey Mackay: This entrepreneur, number-one *New
York Times* best-selling author and motivational
speaker built a fledgling Minnesota envelope company into a giant, thanks to a positive sales environment and good customer relations.

■ John Hickenlooper: An unemployed geologist 25
years ago, he had the business vision and gumption
to open brewpubs in decaying downtowns. Today
the successful restaurateur has left the business of
food to others while he helms the city of Denver,
Colorado, as its mayor.

■ Jerry Shereshewsky: This international advertising/
marketing genius and entrepreneur is renowned for
taking on the competition. He has more than 35 years
experience creating strategies for the biggest and best.

His credits include helping to bring to market products such as Mello-Yello (soft drinks), Gevalia (coffee), and now Grandparents.com (*www.grandparents.com*).

Additional tips throughout the book will come from more of the business world's heaviest hitters, including:

- Patricia Miller: The co-founder and co-president of the wildly successful Vera Bradley women's accessories offer insights into some of what it takes to transform an entrepreneurial idea into a success story.

- Fess Parker: After playing both Davy Crockett and Daniel Boone on television, he developed his business acumen, capitalized on opportunities, surrounded himself with experts, and, with his vision and persistence, is now a successful restaurateur, vintner, and hotelier.

- Jon Nordmark: With a far-reaching vision of the Internet as the perfect sales channel, he gambled everything in pursuit of his dream and founded eBags, today the largest online retailer of luggage, purses, and more.

- David Peterson: Without innovation and vision, Peterson's father, Herb, never would have come up with McDonald's venerable Egg McMuffin. The younger Peterson carries on the tradition of innovation today.

Whether yours is a tiny business struggling to grow or an already successful small business looking to maintain its edge, or you simply aspire for your business to be the best in its field, *Battling Big Box* can help. We'll provide the tools you'll need to balance all aspects of your business and make them work for long-term success.

The book is divided into two parts:

1. **Part I: The Battle Lines Are Drawn:** why small businesses can succeed against mega-sized competition, and what it takes to do so.

2. **Part II: The Plan of Attack:** step-by-step how you can take your business to the next level and ensure its long-term success.

Throughout the book we also include quick checklists, directions, and explanations of how and where to go for more information and help, along with the chapter roundups of tips to success called More Ammunition. The latter can help small business owner/operators see how their own businesses stack up against the mega-competition, and how to make up for any shortcomings. Additionally, in the *From the Trenches* section, in each chapter coauthor Dubroff shares some of his experiences building a successful company. These are excerpts from his notebooks that chronicle the growth of the *Pacific Coast Business Times*.

If you're ready to get your business—whether it's new, well-established, somewhere in between, or simply a dream and an idea—on the right track to success, turn the page and let's get started.

PART

I

THE BATTLE LINES
ARE DRAWN

CHAPTER
1

THE POWER OF SMALL

A business is a series of calamities waiting to happen. It is the job of management to anticipate as many as possible and head them off, then cope with the ones that can't be anticipated.

—Joe Nida, attorney, business advisor, Santa Barbara, California

Move over, Big Box retailers, multinational conglomerates, global manufacturers, and regional chains, small specialty stores, corner restaurants, business-to-business local service providers, and micro-manufacturers aren't going away. In fact, they're becoming an even bigger thorn in your side, sometimes even changing the way you do business, and enjoying their successes all the way to the bank.

Every day tens of thousands of niche businesses can and do compete successfully in today's global marketplace packed with mega-sized competitors. Some of those small businesses crush their competition, and some become a Big Box themselves!

Small Businesses' Big Clout

A small business typically is defined as an independent business with fewer than 500 employees. Of the 26.8 million businesses in the United States in 2006, 5.9 million of those have employees and the rest are one-person operations that may rely on contract workers, according to statistics and analysis from the U.S. Small Business Administration Office of Advocacy.[1] Together these small businesses power the U.S. economy.

■ ■ ■ ■ ■ ■ ■ ■ ■ ■ ■ ■ ■

The Power of Small

Small businesses in the United States pack plenty of punch, as reflected by statistics from the U.S. Small Business Administration:

■ *Small businesses account for more than 99 percent of all employer firms in the United States.*

■ *These businesses employ about half of all the employees in the private sector.*

■ *Firms with fewer than 20 employees account for 31.2 million workers (U.S. Department of Commerce, Census Bureau).*

■ *Throughout the past decade, small businesses provide 60 to 80 percent of the net new jobs annually. In 2004 (the most recent data available), small firms accounted for ALL of the net new jobs. A net new job refers to new jobs in excess of the number of lost jobs.*

■ *Small businesses pay out close to half (45 percent) of total U.S. private payroll of $4.5 trillion.[2]*

■ *These small companies hire 40 percent of high-tech workers, including scientists, engineers, and computer workers.*

■ *They also make up 97 percent of the exporters and produce 28.6 percent of the known export value (fiscal year 2004).*

Source: U.S. Small Business Administration Office of Advocacy.[3]

■ ■ ■ ■ ■ ■ ■ ■ ■ ■ ■ ■

Starts and Closures of Employer Firms 2002–2006

Category	2002	2003	2004	2005	2006
New Firms	569,750	612,296	628,917	653,100*	649,700*
Closures	586,890	540,658	541,047	543,700*	564,900*
Bankruptcies	38,540	35,037	34,317	39,201	19,695**

*Estimate (*www.sba.gov/advo/research/rs258tot.pdf*)

Source: U.S. Department of Commerce, Bureau of the Census; Administrative Office of the U.S. Courts; U.S. Department of Labor, Employment and Training (*http://app1.sba.gov/faqs/faqindex.cfm?areaID=24*)[4]

The biggest mistake many small businesses make is thinking of themselves as small, says Martha Rogers, PhD, founding partner of Peppers & Rogers Group and coauthor of *Rules to Break and Laws to Follow: How Your Business Can Beat the Crisis of Short-Termism* (Wiley, 2008). "As a result, their owners think they cannot compete with bigger companies, and therefore they don't try," says Rogers. "Instead, they should be looking at the opportunities they have to beat large businesses at their own games."

The *Secret* to Success

The *secret* to achieving and sustaining long-term success for a small business isn't really a *secret*; the formula isn't proprietary, and you don't have to ante up cash to a Website, motivational guru, or 800 number. Of course we can't absolutely guarantee that, with it your business will succeed, but we can almost guarantee that without it, your business won't. It's really quite simple, and people pay lip service to it all the time, too. Nonetheless, in reality its execution is often overlooked by small-business owners/operators with dire consequences.

■ ■ ■ ■ ■ ■ ■ ■ ■ ■

Five Essentials for Business Success

A small business needs all five of the following essentials aligned and working together to create and sustain long-term success:

1. *Employee empowerment.*
2. *Effective branding.*
3. *Your customers and effective sales.*
4. *Control over your cash.*
5. *Vision that leads to innovation.*

■ ■ ■ ■ ■ ■ ■ ■ ■ ■

To maintain and grow long term, you as a small-business owner/operator must take a dynamic multitasking approach to the five essential parts of your business. All five parts must work together consistently at all times in order for the business to adapt to market changes. Otherwise, the risk of failure is huge. Those five essential ingredients of any business include:

1. The human element: finding and developing employees you can count on.
2. Branding: creating the right company and product image, and then advertising to get the message out and bring in customers.
3. Your customers and sales: a business needs customers and a strategy to grow sales.
4. Financial management: keeping track of and maintaining a company's cash flow.
5. Vision, innovation, and forward thinking for long-term success.

Without any one of these parts, and all parts working in sync with the others, a small business simply can't maintain momentum and compete through the long haul. That sounds clear enough, and it is. Unfortunately, the execution—or lack of—can cause major trouble. Typically, entrepreneurs who start businesses excel in only one or two of these areas, and not all five. A small-business owner, for example, can be a sales whiz or marketing genius who is great with customers and employees, but just can't get the number-crunching right. Or perhaps an entrepreneur has revolutionary ideas for products and presentation, but is a lousy one-on-one communicator.

Many people assume they can handle the parts of their business that they're not the expert in, or that if they get one part right, the others will fall in line no problem. But that just doesn't happen, and these small business owners/operators are not prepared for or educated in what it takes to truly operate all aspects of the business successfully and long term.

If, however, you identify your shortcomings up-front, it's usually possible to make up for them with the help of the right advisors and employees. If you don't, you'll likely become just one more out-of-business-for-whatever-reason statistic.

Success and Longevity

Every year about 625,000 small businesses figuratively open their doors, and a slightly smaller number close theirs. That's the norm no matter the economy or what's happening in the nation's business cycle, according to Brian Headd, an economist with the U.S. Small Business Administration Office of Advocacy and an expert on small-business economics.

That means if you have a business today, there's a 10 percent chance your business won't be around next year. "That doesn't mean it's a failure. It just means it won't be operating in a year," says Headd.

About half of all small business starts survive four years or more. The other half go away for one reason or another, he adds. Those numbers have been consistent for the past 20 years or so. A small business could close, for example, because its owner/operator gets a great job offer or has health issues, or simply elects to move on to a new challenge.

"It's tough to generalize why small businesses fail. To do that, you're trying to generalize about 600,000 companies, and that's not the easiest thing to do," says Headd. "In some cases I don't even know if the owner knows why the business fails."

According to the Bureau of Labor Statistics, 66 percent of new establishments remain in existence after two years, and only 44 percent after four years across all sectors of industry. That includes manufacturing, an industry often assumed to be declining![5]

Failure Is an Option

At least a portion of those businesses that close file for bankruptcy. In 12 months, from September 2006 to September 2007, nearly 26,000 businesses of all sizes filed for bankruptcy in the U.S. Bankruptcy Courts.[6] That's down from 31,562 in fiscal year 2006. However changes in bankruptcy laws also affect those numbers.[7]

Businesses cite various reasons for their bankruptcies. According to one major study for the SBA Business Bankruptcy Project[8], they include:

- 38.5 percent: outside business conditions such as new competition or increased cost of doing business including increases in rent or insurance, declining real estate values, or other prices.

- 28 percent: financing problems such as high-debt service, loss of financing, or inability to get financing.

- 27.1 percent: inside business conditions, which can include mismanagement, decline in production, bad location, loss of major client, and the inability to collect accounts receivable.

- 20.1 percent: tax issues such as problems with the IRS or state or local tax officials.

- 18.8 percent: disputes with a creditor such as foreclosures, contract disputes, lawsuits, collection disputes, and more.

- 16.9 percent: personal issues of the small-business owner including illness and divorce.

- 9.6 percent: calamities such as fraud, theft by an outsider, natural disasters, accidents at the company, and restricted business access due to road construction, for example.

- 6.4 percent: other reasons including trying to sell the business, involuntary bankruptcy, and buying time.

Though released 10 years ago, the study's findings still are quoted extensively today and provide a snapshot of issues small businesses face every day.

Overlooked Advantages

Whatever the reasons listed, high on the list of troubles for many small businesses is the fact that many owners/operators fail to capitalize on their biggest advantage—small size and agility. When consumers' tastes suddenly change, new technologies enter the market, markets shift, employees quit, or outside forces prompt the need for change, a small business can react quickly. The Big Box competition can't, period. It's that simple.

From the Trenches

Sales are the lifeblood of a business. When, without warning, I lost half of the two-man sales team at my small business—the *Pacific Coast Business Times*, an independent business journal in Southern California—I had plenty of reason to panic. Instead, George, our sales manager, and I started looking for potential replacements. When we found the right person, I hired him on the spot—no other executives to confer with, no board approval required, no questions from anyone else. It felt right, so we did it. It's that simple. The decision was ours alone, and we did it all in one day. As a small business, and unlike the mega-competition in the Los Angeles metropolitan area, I don't have layers of management to consult, elaborate corporate protocols to follow, or lengthy hiring hoops to jump through— all of which are standard operating procedures for giant corporations no matter the industry.

If the toddler/tween fashion trend in Middle America, specifically Indianapolis, Indiana, goes tie-dye overnight, so can Jackie Pantella's store window display. She's the owner-operator of Little Women, a single-location children's apparel specialty retailer that's been in business for nearly 15 years. Pantella quickly can switch her store's window display to reflect the fleeting fad, and then make calls to line up more backup product if necessary. At her chain-store Big Box competition, on the other hand, it's a different story. Fad or not, no window displays change because they are dictated by corporate headquarters. Small has B-I-G advantages!

Small Trumps Big

Small businesses may fail, but so do the Big Boxes on the block, some because they underestimate the power of small. Almost daily we hear tales of yet another Big Box in trouble. Venerable giants in the world of business-to-business, and well-known names in the business-to-consumer world—such as CompUSA, Sharper Image, Montgomery Ward, and Mrs. Fields (of cookie fame)—have disappeared or been forced to face up to the threat of extinction and regroup. Even if a Big Box doesn't totally fail, its business practices often come up short, and the company must regroup or reinvent itself. In some cases it's the direct result of small-business successes that change the way the world does business.

Stalwarts such as Dell Computer, Ann Taylor, Gap, and even Walt Disney stores have had to slash workforces, close stores, and regroup. When Wal-Mart Inc. joined the supermarket fray with its supercenters, and the Costcos and Sam's Clubs of the world rose to prominence, the nation's typical Big Box supermarket chains figured they needed to follow the bigger-is-better idea, too. The error of that wisdom eventually translated into sagging bottom lines and bankruptcies. The survivors have since regrouped, and now build or refurbish big stores to look small!

Small Firms Make Big Waves

In the virtual, Internet world, to call the once-small business craigslist.org (*www.craigslist.org*) a success is an understatement. The online discussion forums and classified ads marketplace exemplifies how a niche and an idea to serve it can become a small business that in turn mushrooms into a powerhouse that changes the rules of the game. Today, you can click on one of more than 500 Craigslist.org city sites worldwide, and you can join all kinds of forums or find free or low-cost classifieds for everything from animals to bottles, cash to roommates, widgets, work, and more. Craigslist gets more than 12 billion page views per month. (A page view is a measure of Internet traffic that is defined as one unique person opening a page on the Website one time.)

Craig, as in founder Craig Newmark, and CEO Jim Buckmaster, who helms the company, have made their behemoth the Big Box on the Web and the standard against which other companies compete online and off when it comes to classified advertising. Its business model of low- and no-cost ads is a big part of what's driving traditional print classified advertising venues out of business. Today eBay is a minority shareholder in craigslist.org.

But Craigslist certainly didn't start out as the big kid on the block, and its founder never envisioned that either, back then or even now. Newmark, self-described as a pocket-protector-wearing, hard-core Java and Web programmer in thick black glasses—a nerd, to be exact—started Craigslist as a hobby in early 1995 to fill an underserved niche. He wanted to connect people in San Francisco and get the word out about cool or useful events in the San Francisco Bay Area. Even as Craigslist became THE place nationally to find advertisements for the best tech jobs and job applicants nationwide, postings on the site remained free or very low cost. Back then few even realized there was a "Craig" behind Craigslist.

The site utilized anonymous e-mail relay software, then a relatively new concept that allowed on-site postings of jobs, events, items for sale, and more that did not include direct contact information. Instead, the contact was made through Craigslist. "It's not rocket science," says Newmark, "but I think it was a feature that really did help us grow."

Another marketplace-altering small business is Kinko's, the once-tiny copy shop business that grew to more than 1,500 locations and more than 21,000 employees ("team members") in 21 countries before its founder, Paul Orfalea, sold it to FedEx Corporation in 2004. In 1970, Orfalea started a tiny company near the University of California-Santa Barbara campus with the idea of providing low-cost copies with customer service. Today, you would be hard-pressed to find a copy store with anything less.

Not every small business turns into—nor, for that matter does its owner want to turn it into—the next Kinko's or Craigslist. But each successful small business does change the competitive battlefield, even if only for other small businesses and their customers, and even if only slightly. With every new small business that appears on the scene to fill a new niche or supply a general audience, the competitive battlefield changes. When Sam Addoms and his investor team launched an upstart airline named Frontier Airlines in Denver in 1994, airline travelers in that city suddenly had another transportation option; marketing outlets had another potential source of revenue; nonprofit organizations another source of funding; and so on.

With the launch of the *Pacific Coast Business Times* in Santa Barbara, California, in 1999, other small and large businesses in the area had another advertising venue to target a specific audience. Customers and companies had a choice for their news, and so did advertisers, distributors, manufacturers, and more. We wound up creating a community of businesses in our area that did not exist before. The newspaper's print edition, e-mail, and our sponsored events all work together to give the region a sense of place and an opportunity for companies to connect with nearby markets in ways that previously did not exist. For example, if you were in Ventura and wanted to do business in Santa Maria or Santa Barbara before we came along, your information resources were limited to chamber of commerce mailings and maybe a real estate newsletter generated by a broker. But the *Pacific Coast Business Times* gave and still gives people in the area and the surrounding area something they didn't really have in full before.

Small does make a difference. As a small-business owner or potential owner, don't forget that. You can and do make a difference whether your business succeeds or not.

Fight On!

Why bother to fight? Because you have a good chance to win! That's especially true with today's soft economy, intense competition, and changing business and consumer habits. Whether business-to-business or business-to-consumer, the marketplace is littered with Big Boxes that have succumbed to or at the very least been forced, under threat of extinction, to reinvent themselves. Their demise usually is the result of a number of factors, including their size and inability to pay attention to their market and their customers, and react quickly in turn.

Corpses and Apparitions

Once seemingly untouchable PC behemoth CompUSA, for example, basically was run out of towns coast to coast by its competition. Longtime dominant coffee powerhouse Starbucks is on the run and scrambling to reinvent and survive in the wake of challenges from growing small-business upstarts such as California-based Coffee, Bean and Tea, New York–based Daz Bog, and all the small purveyors of java found in virtually any neighborhood.

Basically these Big Boxes paid too much attention to getting bigger and forgot their neighborhood or core customers.

■ ■ ■ ■ ■ ■ ■ ■ ■ ■ ■

The Untouchables Aren't!

Even venerable companies and their brands are no longer safe from changing market demands. Seemingly every week, we hear of another stalwart in trouble and fading fast. Some of those companies that face or have faced big problems recently are:

■ **IBM:** *The likes of PC-makers Hewlett-Packard and more tamed main-frame giant Big Blue into changing its ways to survive.*

■ **Countrywide Financial Corporation:** *Crippled by its huge sub-prime mortgage portfolio, the once-powerhouse was acquired by Bank of America in 2008.*

■ **Starbucks:** *Under pressure from the competition and the economy, the embattled coffee purveyor announced in 2008 that it will close 600 stores.*

■ **Gap Inc.:** *The owner of Gap, Banana Republic, and Old Navy caved in to the competition in 2008 and announced it would close more than 100 stores in an effort to survive.*

■ **Mrs. Fields Famous Brands LLC:** *The seller of those tasty chocolate chip cookies and TCBY yogurt is among the latest to face the possibility of extinction. The company filed for Chapter 11 bankruptcy protection in August 2008.*

■ **Aloha Airgroup:** *The owner of Aloha Airlines, the second-largest air carrier in Hawaii, filed for bankruptcy in 2008, citing competition as a big reason for its demise.*

Other 2008 bankruptcies include: S and A Restaurant Corporation, owner of Bennigan's and Steak and Ale, and Frontier Airlines.

■ ■ ■ ■ ■ ■ ■ ■ ■ ■ ■

And what about the online banking industry? Fifteen years ago, the idea of banking through a computer sounded out of the question to most Americans. Today, four out of 10, or 40 percent, of Americans rely on that convenience, and that's up 25 percent from 2005, according to research from the Pew Internet and American Life Project.[9]

Forget the Excuses

Don't buy the "that was then; this is now" excuse for not following your own small-business dreams, either. It's all about finding the right niche, making the commitment, taking the right approach, and the execution. Craigslist's Newmark, Kinkos' Orfalea, and plenty of others didn't give in or give up. They all made the choice to start a small business, struggled through its ups and downs, faced the crises, conquered them, and persevered.

You never know where you might find your right niche, or what that niche might be. Would you ever think purses and bags could be a new and different niche? Patricia Miller and Barbara Bradley Baekgaard were in the Atlanta airport waiting for a plane home from a Florida vacation when the friends noticed that female travelers had the same drab canvas carry-on luggage as their male counterparts. "We were talking and decided that women would like carry-on bags, but they should be attractive and feminine and pretty," says Miller.

When they returned to their homes in Fort Wayne, Indiana, the designing duo came up with the idea for a soft, brightly colored, quilted duffel bag, bought fabric, made some prototypes, and soon sold them out at an in-home ladies apparel party. Phenom startup Vera Bradley was born. From its small in-home beginnings, the company today is an international power in the women's accessories market, and its brightly colored cloth products are instantly recognizable.

A hat is a hat is a hat—at least that's what most of us tend to think. Don't tell Rick White that. He's president and CEO of

Imperial Headwear, which makes custom hats—the embroidered caps with visors worn by athletes and the rest of us—and more. The Colorado-based micro-manufacturer has been producing its high-end specialty hats for more than 90 years. That's small-business niche success. "Basically we have identified segments of the business that the big (box) companies prefer not to service, and we have found a way to do it profitably," says White.

Everyday Battles

Starting a small business is tough, and operating it is no picnic, either. Just ask anyone who has done it—successfully or not. It's like navigating a small boat on a big ocean: Most of the time the sea is relatively smooth, but storms can come up suddenly. With the right skills (and a little luck) you can survive the storm, and seas will return to their idyllic calm (chaos). With a business, large or small problems can happen all at once. Survival depends on your skills and ability to move quickly and alleviate those problems so that calm returns. Joe Nida, a corporate attorney in Santa Barbara, California, now deceased, had some great advice for entrepreneurs. The gruff transplanted New Yorker liked to observe that a business was a series of disasters waiting to happen. It was the job of its management to anticipate as many as possible, head them off, and then cope with the ones that actually hit.

In case you think that sounds overly fatalistic, consider the events of one day recently at the *Pacific Coast Business Times*: Our new Website failed to launch properly; one of our two lead advertising salespeople—that's 50 percent of the ad revenue-generating staff—abruptly quit; the owner of an area hotel (and advertiser) was unhappy with a story in the paper and hired an attorney to "investigate" possible libel; and naturally this happened on the day the newspaper was slated to go to press. All I wanted to do that morning was to telephone in the payroll, celebrate our publisher's birthday, and get ready for a long weekend vacation in Colorado.

Unfortunately, the business necessitated something else. We were able to quickly restore the Website and to locate a seasoned advertising sales pro to pinch-hit on the ad desk until we could find a replacement. The unhappy hotel owner was left to deal with our libel lawyers. But that's the way things go even in a well-established, profitable business.

Victory Without a Battle? Dream On!

Let's look at a few statistics from the NFIB Research Foundation, part of NFIB (the National Federation of Independent Business), which surveyed small employers—those with one to 250 employees—about their competition. Among the results of the 2003 survey:[10]

- 53 percent of small-business owners describe their current competitive climate as highly competitive; 28 percent say it's competitive; and 61 percent says it's much more competitive than three years ago.

- 57 percent of small businesses typically compete against a mix of large and small firms; 28 percent say it's principally other small organizations; and 13 percent say the main competition is large companies.

- 49 percent of small businesses say their principal competition is within 10 miles of their business; another 26 percent says it's within 100 miles; and only 4 percent indicate that it originates outside the United States.

Finding the niche was easy for Paul Holstein. It was the everyday ups and downs that were tough for CableOrganizer.com. Six years ago Paul Holstein didn't know what home-based business he was going to start or the niche he might find. He only knew that his pregnant wife, Valerie, needed to work after their first child was born, and she wanted to stay home with the baby. So Paul, a CPA doing full-time financial consulting on enterprise resource planning systems, along with Valerie, set about furnishing a home office. "We bought a glass desk and set it up. But it looked terrible because you could see this tangled mass of cables and wires, and some cords were actually tripping hazards" says Holstein. "So, figuring somebody must have the solution, I typed into my computer the URL *www.cableorganizer.com*. To my surprise, nothing came up so I turned to my wife and said, 'That's the company we're going to start.'"

Holstein had found a niche and decided to capitalize on it. At first he and his wife operated the company out of their garage. But as the company outgrew that space, Holstein figured the next step had to be a storefront, so they rented a 2,000-square-foot facility in a shopping center. Big mistake! The location was wrong, and their products weren't exactly conducive to the browsing shopper. In fact, the few shoppers who wandered in did little more than disrupt Holstein's ability to serve phone customers. Holstein swallowed the loss, and the company moved on to warehouse facilities. Today, more than 150,000 customers later, *www.cableorganizer.com* has 44 employees, an inventory of more than 17,000 items, and more than $10 million in annual sales.

Big Box in Perspective

The marketplace, for both businesses and consumers, and across all industries, is to some extent overwhelmed with Big Box competition. That's a given. What isn't as widely understood by entrepreneurs is that those Big Box providers aren't necessarily your greatest competition or your biggest problem. A few million dollars in sales—the lifeblood and likely prosperity for your small business—means little in the billion- and sometimes even trillion-dollar economics of truly giant Big Boxes. Working you and your business into a frenzy to compete with WalMart won't get you anywhere. You can't win one on one, period! That's given. With the power of small innovation and vision, you can employ guerrilla tactics and whittle away at the Big Box's sales.

■ ■ ■ ■ ■ ■ ■ ■ ■ ■ ■

As a small business, your main direct competition is other small businesses.
—Brian Headd, economist, Office of Advocacy, U.S. Small Business Administration

■ ■ ■ ■ ■ ■ ■ ■ ■ ■ ■

In the retail sector, for example, if a Walmart opens down the street, a small business can't realistically compete with the same merchandise on the same level, says Martin Lehman, a business counselor and marketing director for SCORE in New York. (SCORE, a partner with the SBA, is a national nonprofit association with volunteers who work with entrepreneurs to help them grow their small businesses.)

Just because Walmart comes to town doesn't mean you're going out of business, either, says Lehman. They can bring customers to town, too, so as a small business owner/operator, you must look for a way to differentiate yourself in your niche. With clothes, that might mean carrying different product labels that perhaps are more up-to-date, fashionable, or of better quality, adds Lehman, also a former entrepreneur with a small chain of apparel stores in the Midwest.

As a small business, your main direct competition, instead, is other small businesses, says SBA's Headd. Those are the companies that target the same customers—whether businesses or consumers—with similar niche products and services, and can derail even the best entrepreneurial efforts.

Here are a few more results of that NFIB survey:

- ■ 57 percent of small businesses typically compete against a mix of large and small firms; 28 percent; compete principally against other small organizations, and 13 percent say they compete principally against large ones.

- 12 percent of small-business owners say a Big Box store or a large chain store is a significant competitor; 13 percent say they're a marginal competitor; 8 percent report that businesses outside the United States are significant competitors; and 9 percent say that they are marginal competitors.

- More than 80 percent of small businesses say the major strategies they use to compete are to provide the highest possible quality and better service.

- Other less-important ways small businesses compete (from the most used to the least) are minimizing overhead; maximizing the use of technology; targeting missed or poorly served customers; offering more choices and selection, unique marketing, lower prices, expansion or growth, a superior location, new or previously unavailable goods and services, alliances or cooperation with another firm or firms; and franchising.

Your Ammunition

Some essentials to remember from this chapter include:

- Small businesses carry plenty of economic clout, accounting for more than 99 percent of all employer firms, and half of all private-sector employees in the United States.

- The five essentials for long-term small business success include employee empowerment; effective branding; customers and a path to grow sales; control over your cash; and vision that leads to innovation.

- Operating a small business isn't easy, but it can be extremely rewarding. Just be prepared with the skills and ability to move quickly to alleviate problems.

■ Don't sweat the plethora of Walmarts and the like. You can't compete one on one, dollar for dollar, period. With the power of small innovation and vision, you can employ guerrilla tactics and whittle away at the Big Box's sales.

CHAPTER
2

MOMENTS OF TRUTH: CAN YOU CUT IT?

If you have not had your panic attack this week, you are not paying attention.

—George Wolverton, publisher, *Pacific Coast Business Times*

Going out on your own, especially in mid-life or mid-career, can be risky. And the risks never go away. In fact, with success they often are compounded. Even if you own an already-established small business that dominates its niche, you regularly face tough decisions and truths that place your future and that of your business on the line. It's a mid-life crisis on steroids, only it happens regardless of your age.

The ownership alternative isn't for everybody. Owning a business isn't easy and requires mammoth time and efforts; as we talked about in the last chapter, your odds of success or failure over the long haul are about even. But on good days it's unbelievably liberating to run your own show.

"There has never been a day that I do not enjoy coming to work," says entrepreneur Jackie Pantella. "Some days you have more hassles than others, but I love going to work."

Perhaps that attitude toward being your own boss is why there are so many millions of small-business owners in the United States. In 2007, a total of 495,000 new businesses launched each month, with 300 of every 100,000 adults involved in the startup process, according to the Kauffman Index of Entrepreneurial Activity from the nonprofit Kansas City, Missouri–based Ewing Marion Kauffman Foundation.[1] The national assessment is an annual study to measure business startup activity for the entire United States adult population at the individual owner level.

"At a time when the nation is concerned about the economy, it is heartening to see that entrepreneurial activity continues to rise," says Carl Schramm, Foundation president and chief executive officer. "The entrepreneurial sector is a critical factor in our nation's economic growth. Even during times of recession, new firms have been responsible for the bulk of new jobs and innovations in America. That is why it is vital to track startup trends like we track other economic indicators."

From the Trenches

I started the *Pacific Coast Business Times*, a weekly business journal, in 1999 with a leased Saab, my checkbook, a business plan, roughly $400,000 in financial backing, and a drive to be my own boss. I still have the Saab and the checkbook. The business plan, now a bit dusty, is still a good read. But making the transition from working for a big corporation as editor of a business journal to owner of my own newspaper didn't exactly happen overnight and without headaches and hassles, as well as help and guidance from others.

The drive to become your own boss and the exhilaration, freedom, and satisfaction associated with it is a familiar tune among entrepreneurs. Nearly nine out of 10 entrepreneurs are upbeat about their choice of careers, according to the 2008 American Express OPEN Small Business Monitor, a semi-annual survey of business owners.[2] A few more insights from that survey include:

- 86 percent of entrepreneurs describe themselves as seeing "the glass half full."

- 49 percent of business owners like the fact that being an entrepreneur allows them to maintain the quality of life they want.

- 75 percent would recommend entrepreneurship to a family member or friend.

- 74 percent recommend that their child become an entrepreneur.

Are you willing to take the plunge, dream big, and go for it? If so, get ready for headaches, heartaches, struggle, and disappointment—along with the satisfaction of owning your own business and being your own boss.

Fortunately, though, if you are aware of and understand many of the pitfalls up-front, you can take steps ahead of time to soften the bumps and lessen your chances of failure. Let's look more closely at some of the bumps and at what motivates others to give up solid jobs for the exuberance/headache of small-business ownership.

The Real Deal

In these days of soaring costs across the board, most of us are constantly looking for ways to make an extra buck. Home offices are the norm, and a big chunk of Americans dabble in part-time or contract work on the side. But even hanging out a shingle with your business's name on it, filing a Schedule C (business income/loss) tax form with the Internal Revenue Service, and saying you're in business for yourself is different from truly taking the plunge to become an owner/operator of a small business with a payroll and all the responsibilities associated with it. We're talking about making the decision to start a company, finding the right niche, laying out a formal business plan, identifying funding sources, hiring staff, and then taking it all to the next level.

Fear and Perseverance

Whether you're just starting out, already in business, or either plodding along or losing ground to you competition, you always can find plenty of reasons to throw in the towel, call it quits, or simply accept the fact that your small business can't possibly compete against its rivals—either Big Box or fellow small business. But you can compete and win with the right vision, approach, and execution.

Well-known actor and television star Fess Parker, who played both Davy Crockett and Daniel Boone in successful television series, retired from acting in 1970. Accustomed to playing the role of a tough frontiersman, he set out on his own new frontier. As a boy, he had picked up some knowledge of real-estate from his dad, who had dabbled in the Texas real estate market in the 1930s. So Parker purchased some small rental properties in Santa Barbara, California, and launched a new career. Eventually he moved 30 miles north to the Santa Ynez Valley, where he could grow grapes for wine. Today the Fess Parker Winery and Vineyards is renowned.

Meanwhile, Parker had other big ideas, too. He seized the opportunity to get an option to buy a nearly abandoned railroad yard in the area. He brought in a financial partner, and Fess Parker's Doubletree Resort became reality. The old train yard's roundhouse was the inspiration for a large open air rotunda in the hotel.

But Parker wasn't done yet. In 2008, he broke ground on a smaller luxury hotel near the Doubletree. What is significant about the groundbreaking was that he waited more than 10 years for the permit to do so! That's vision, persistence, and guts.

From the Trenches

When I decided to trade a job as an editor of someone else's publication for the helm of my own newspaper, I, like many others who jump from a sound and familiar ship to an unfamiliar, possibly leaky one, was petrified of failure. My fear was a very real possibility, too, considering my vision of the *Pacific Coast Business Times* involved serving a portion of the Los Angeles metropolitan area. Papers already in the area included venerable publishing giants such as the *Los Angeles Times* and the *Ventura County Star*, as well as the more moderately sized *Santa Barbara News Press*, and smaller dailies such as the *San Luis Obispo Tribune*, *Santa Maria Times*, and the *Lompoc Record*. That doesn't even include the dozens of small weeklies and alternative newspapers that pepper the area. I would wake up at 3 a.m. and worry, worry, worry about all the horrible things that could happen.

It wasn't necessarily the Big Boxes, however, that scared me. I was terrified that one of the extremely tiny competitors that had cropped up to serve a business audience in our area could be bought by a larger company and turned into a real rival. For that reason I was driven to buy the strongest of the little business publications in our area, the *Business Digest*, and get its assets on our balance sheet before we ever launched the *Pacific Coast Business Times*.

Joyce Meskis was a cash-poor divorcee looking for a job in the book business in 1974, when it just so happened that the tiny Tattered Cover Book Store in the upscale Cherry Creek area of Denver, Colorado, went up for sale. She approached the owner about buying it. He wanted a lot of money for the 3-year-old store, says Meskis. "I had no money. That was the bad news. The good news

was the owner didn't want much money down, and the even better news was that he was willing to carry the note. So I scraped up
the down payment by tapping my friends and relatives, and made
an offer, which was promptly rejected. He said somebody else had
made a better offer. Some time went by and a friend of mine said,
'Why don't you go back and see what happened with the Tattered
Cover?' I'm sure he would have come back to me if things had
fallen through—I'm a quiet person; I don't push. And my friend
said, 'Well you ought to go check.' So I did, and sure enough the
deal had fallen through. Lesson Number 439 in life: perseverance!" says Meskis.

■ ■ ■ ■ ■ ■ ■ ■ ■ ■

Lesson Number 439 in life: perseverance.

— Joyce Meskis, owner of the Tattered Cover bookstore, Denver,
Colorado

■ ■ ■ ■ ■ ■ ■ ■ ■ ■

She borrowed more money from more people; her offer was
accepted, and the Tattered Cover era under Meskis had begun.
Seven expansions of the original store, and multiple moves later,
she has turned Tattered Cover into one of the largest independent
bookstores in the country with three locations in the metropolitan
area. Meskis accomplished her legendary success through a com-
bination of perseverance, unparalleled customer service, vision, and
unflinching dedication. (At one point in 2000, she even went to
court to uphold the First Amendment rights of her customers.
Despite a search warrant, she refused to release sales records related to a customer in a criminal case. That case ended up in the
Colorado Supreme Court, and eventually Meskis won.)

Her small business endurance, however, hasn't been easy and
still isn't, she insists, and she's had her share of bumps in the road.
Big Box–heavy discount competition has been fierce throughout
the years from the likes of Crown Books (a former discounter out
of Washington, D.C.), Barnes & Noble, Borders, B. Dalton/

Pickwick Books (now a division of Barnes & Noble), Walden Books (now a division of Borders), and, of course, the Internet. "We are enduring," says Meskis. "We're in a very tough business, and that has been true from the beginning and it's especially true now. The jury is always out in this business life. A lot of our colleagues—longtime ones—have closed. The future and people's crystal balls are pretty cloudy right now."

The definition of success, however, for Meskis, doesn't necessarily mean fancy trappings such as mountain homes and private jets: "I think (success) is that we have been able to do business in a way that we think is important to our community. We have done it in a way that we believe is ethical and encouraging of the culture of our society, and I hope we've raised a few critical thinkers in our lives."

Plenty of other places in the country have their own local small business icons and visionaries similar to Meskis. In Southern California, that icon is Paul Orfalea, founder of what once was a tiny copy store grounded in providing top-notch customer service and taking care of its employees. That company was Kinko's. Before FedEx Corporation acquired it in 2004, Orfalea had grown that single copy store into a Big Box with 23,000 employees and 1,500 outlets worldwide. By then some things had changed, and some hadn't. When Orfalea opened his first store in 1970, it was near the University of California in Santa Barbara and occupied such a tiny space that in order to use the copier, it had to be dragged outside in front of the store. Orfalea's idea was simple. Similar to Meskis and Tattered Cover, he targeted a special niche—in this case college students looking for products and services they needed at a competitive price. And, similar to what by then was the larger Tattered Cover, he executed that service very well.

Rules of the Road

Obviously big ideas and dreams alone don't translate into small-business success. It takes much more—from choosing the right niche to putting together the necessary financing, smart execution, and the list goes on. All the parts of the business must work together smoothly, too, day in and day out. If one part is out of sync or out of place, your business dreams and goals can come crashing down.

Choose Your Niche Wisely

We previously talked about Paul and Valerie Holstein, who started their home business called CableOrganizer.com. They had only meager savings, and Paul worked a day job when they launched their company in January 2002. "I was working full time, our garage was the warehouse, and my wife fulfilled orders," says Holstein.

Warehouse space and his day job weren't the problems, however. Customers and price points were. The Holsteins had chosen a niche with four basic products that were relatively inexpensive—less than $20 each—and hadn't invested enough in search engine optimization to generate enough business from Day 1. Search engine optimization relates to the order in which an online search tool displays its results. In the case of CableOrganizer.com, when a potential buyer searched for a product to organize his or her computer cables, CableOrganizer.com wasn't among the top few listed. The end result, says Holstein, "We had one sale in April, five sales in May and 30 sales in June 2002. We didn't have any extra money to hire someone to generate sales for us, so when I would get home at night I studied and studied about search engine optimization."

■ ■ ■ ■ ■ ■ ■ ■

Remember, a sale is a sale is a sale.
Could I have found another niche that would have had a higher price point or would have had more traffic?
—Paul Holstein, CableOrganizer.com

■ ■ ■ ■ ■ ■ ■ ■

Obviously his studies worked, because today the company thrives. But in retrospect, Holstein has a few ideas. "This is a great niche, but if I could start over, I might have considered whether there was another niche with a higher price point," he says.

Whether dealing with business-to-business or business-to-consumer products and services, if you're looking for a niche to either start a new company or energize an existing one, some questions—and their answers—to consider include:

- Is there a market for the product or service?
- Is the market big enough to sustain your company's growth and development?
- Is the cost of the product/service (the price point) high enough to generate sufficient income from sales?

And though it wasn't an issue for Holstein's company because he started with only himself and his wife as employees, don't forget to think about whether you have a ready source of employees for your company. That's especially important if, for example, your niche involves manufacturing a product or requires many employees—a call center or production plant perhaps. You can have the greatest product or services, but, if the production plant or service facility is located in a sparsely populated geographic area that doesn't have enough people to staff it, or the available workforce isn't willing to work for the wages you offer, you could be out of luck and your small business headed for demise.

Make sure any potential small-business niche is in a growth business or a growth opportunity if it's a totally new concept, says Jim Wolfe, an entrepreneur and now SCORE counselor in California, who is particularly familiar with success. In 1995, the former executive of Coca-Cola and Welch's led a struggling nutritional bar company and turned it into the Balance Bar powerhouse, which was sold to a Big Box competitor (the largest U.S. food company) five years later, for more than $260 million.

If, for example, one huge competitor already dominates the field you've chosen for your niche, a small business can find it especially challenging to compete and succeed. It's not that it can't be done; it's just not easy and requires perhaps a different approach. Google is an example of a dominant force in a particular niche, which is Internet search engines. To challenge that behemoth would be very tough—unless, of course, you're in partnership with an equally dominant force. Microsoft has taken on Google, but it's a Big Box, too.

"I call it the art and science of 'niche-picking,'" says Harvey Mackay, world-renowned entrepreneur, *New York Times* best-selling author, motivational speaker, and more. At age 26, Mackay bought a fledgling Minnesota company and built it into one of the nation's largest envelope companies, MackayMitchell Envelope Company, which today produces 25 million envelopes a day. He cautions niche-seeking entrepreneurs to beware the four lethal mega-myths about niches:

- **Myth one**: *A niche has to be chic.* Turtle Wax has held a dependable—and sizable—share of the car-wax market for decades. This task is synonymous with something people hate to do. Romantic stuff, huh?

- **Myth two**: *A niche has to be new.* More than 60 percent of the couples in America have abandoned the traditional family structure in which the husband is the only breadwinner. Everyone is chasing the two-income family these days—especially the woman in the workplace. But what about the millions of women in the traditional homemaker role? Only a fool would neglect the power of that still-immense market segment.

- **Myth three**: *A niche shouldn't be too narrow.* Don't assume that because your niche is larger, it's better. Wouldn't you rather be fighting for half of a 28-percent segment than one-seventh of a 44-percent one?

- **Myth four**: *A niche has to be neat.* Not every niche is defined with the sharpness of a surgeon's scalpel.

There are liquor stores in the toniest sections of Manhattan, Chicago's Gold Coast, and Beverly Hills, California, that do as much volume in Chateau Ripple, as Chateau Laffite-Rothschild, vintage 1895. No one, no matter how wealthy, eats caviar and drinks champagne every day. It isn't that the rich can't afford to do it; it's that it gets as boring as anything else if it becomes routine.

"Niches are necessary for all but the most universal marketers," says Mackay. "So, if you can't please everybody, please somebody. But, don't let niches lure you away from job one: The trick is not to fill up a niche; it's to fill up a customer."

Know Your Customers, Competition, and More

Who are other purveyors of your goods or services? Who or what might be your competition in the future? For that matter, what will your product or service look like in the future? (The latter is a part of what we call "vision," and we'll delve more deeply into that in Chapter 7.) These are all questions that need answers, or at least educated guesses, long before you decide to hang out your own shingle. The marketplace coast to coast is littered with corpses of small businesses whose owners didn't really do their homework up-front.

From the Trenches

Before I ever launched the *Pacific Coast Business Times*, I thoroughly researched potential customers, potential advertisers, the geographic location, community needs, and more. I knew there were also a couple of fringe business publications in the market that had the potential to grow into larger competitors. That potential competition in part led me to purchase an existing monthly publication to gain a toehold in the market. When I took over the tiny business publication, the *Business Digest*, it had a subscription list of about 1,500 executives and other movers and shakers, who actually received the paper free. But it was a start. I used that list as a base to launch a serious weekly business journal.

After a year, we began charging for our bigger and better publication. However, we carefully explained its value-added components to our customers and the community. When we finished our "Operation Conversion Storm," half of the free subscribers sent in their subscription checks.

This kind of analysis should be an automatic process for any potential entrepreneur. Even if you're an already-established small business, in order to grow and thrive long-term you must constantly be aware of current and future customers, changing trends, and competitors, and be willing to change to accommodate and adapt to them.

Imperial Headwear's CEO Rick White ran smack into the changing needs of business-to-business customers when he lost a big deal to a golf-course management company about 18 months ago. He recounts the story:

"We called on a management group that controlled more than 200 golf courses and represented significant purchase potential. We walked in and the buyer said, 'A hat is a hat is a hat. We have three vendors. We are going to walk out of this meeting with two. What do you have for us?'

"That attitude is anathema to us. We pride ourselves in our quality, our service, and our fit. When I hear a comment like that, it's somebody who is clearly looking for a low-cost product where they can drive absolute retail margins and that creates a big challenge for us. (In other words, Imperial is not generally the low-cost provider.)

"We didn't get the business. But on the heels of that meeting, we came back and I said, 'Guys, it costs less to buy a cap today than it did 10 years ago. That's a problem for us. What are we going to do about it?'"

What the company did was go back to the drawing board to find products beyond the basic embroidered cap. Imperial began to develop and market what White calls purposeful products—those with a specific role for the wearer, which includes sun protection hats; hats with enhanced moisture-control, fit, and wash ability; and eco-friendly hats—those made from sustainable products.

■ ■ ■ ■ ■ ■ ■ ■ ■

A great idea, a super product, and the right niche alone are NOT enough to guarantee small-business success.

■ ■ ■ ■ ■ ■ ■ ■ ■

The importance of meeting the needs of change aside, White also wisely recognized the value of continuing to serve his core customers. Imperial changed with the times, but did not abandon its traditional product or customer. "Cotton twill will continue to be a large part of our business," says White. "But purpose in our products takes on a whole new importance as we move forward."

Don't assume, though, that, if you have a great idea, a super product, and a great niche, customers will beat down the door as they clamor for your product or services. It takes more for long-term—or even short-term—success, and it's usually one step at a time. Remember that CableOrganizer's Holstein had a great idea and no direct and specialized competition on the Web, but he struggled for customers early on because he hadn't done ALL his homework.

Tattered Cover's Meskis offers an interesting take on what she sees as her company's competition, and it may surprise you.

It's a confluence of circumstances and elements that come together," says Meskis. "I suppose the biggest thing as far as my business goes is that we want people to read. The biggest competitor is the number of other places where people can spend their discretionary income and discretionary time. It's illiteracy; it's a-literacy—people who can read, but don't. That's major competition. Then there's competition within our industry itself," she adds, "and then there's the Internet and changes in technology. You can't stand in the way of the freight train of change. You've got to try and lay the track in the best direction as you see fit. Ours is not just the business. Yes, we are selling a manufactured item—ink on paper between boards—but we're really in the business of ideas. We have to make a business out of it, and to succeed in helping to continue the cultural legacy of our society, yet never lose sight of the fact it's a business. We can't accomplish our philosophical goals if we're out of business.

Prior Experience Counts

The people most likely to succeed in starting up a business are those with experience in that particular field, says Wolfe. "With Balance Bar, the reason why the company wasn't succeeding before I got involved was because they didn't have anybody who had experience in the food business in terms of marketing, sales, and anything relating to that business. They had bright people. That wasn't the issue. When I got involved I had done a lot of this for many years and it was much easier for me to succeed than it would have been for any of them," says Wolfe. "There are obviously some exceptions, but I think if you look at the people who are successful in start ups in small business they each had some kind of grounding in that field. I went to school, so to speak, at Coca-Cola, Welch's, and other companies."

As a SCORE counselor, Wolfe says, he sees many people with great ideas who lack that all-important experience. "If you're entering a field you're not familiar with, get some experience doing it first, or hire out that experience if you can afford to early in the game. Your chances of success are much greater as a result, and I think that applies to just about any small-business opportunity."

One of Wolfe's SCORE clients had an idea for a tea emporium similar to the successful coffee-centered Starbucks concept. It was a great idea, says Wolfe, but the individual never had operated a restaurant. Wolfe advised him to take a part-time job at a local Starbucks to observe and learn how a similar business—Starbucks—executes the business concept properly. Wolfe told the would-be entrepreneur: "Work for them for a couple months and learn their system and how they do it. You'll have access to all that information and then can decide if it's really something you want to do. At least you will learn how to do it right."

Wolfe never heard from the client again. But plenty of successful small businesses are existing proof the concept works.

Children's apparel retailer Pantella agrees. Anyone who owns a small business needs to know where his or her expertise lies, and then figure out the niche that utilizes those talents. Pantella's background in fashion design—she attended a trade school in Philadelphia, Pennsylvania—taught her how to properly fit clothes. She parlayed that expertise into her small business that specializes in sizing children properly for special-occasion clothing.

If you are going to go into business, you had better understand every single aspect of that business, adds Chris Zane, founder and owner of Zane's Cycles, Branford, Connecticut, the largest bicycle shop in Connecticut. Once you become really proficient at understanding the business you're in, then you're not likely to run into any surprises or something you haven't thought through. "I tell my staff the same thing in a different light," says Zane. "We spend 40 hours a week, or 2,000 hours a year, focused on our job. That's a lot of time. If you're going to spend 2,000 hours doing something, you should be really good at it really quickly. To just sit in your business, just doing the busy work, that's not going to get you anywhere. But if you spend 2,000 hours a year learning everything there is to know about the business you are in, you're going to be infinitely more successful."

Keep in mind, too, that it doesn't always take tremendous sums of cash to get started. Sam Hishmeh paid only $1,500 for his first Domino's franchise in Southern California, albeit a failing store on the verge of closing. Nonetheless, it was his start. Incidentally, his second franchise cost him $290,000! The financial strain of that purchase was lessened, Hishmeh says, because he was able to negotiate "great" terms—he had to make a small down payment and the seller carried the rest of the loan. That particular loan has now been paid off for 20 years, he adds.

Tattered Cover's Meskis encountered a somewhat similar situation with a modest down payment and seller-carried financing when she initially bought the bookstore. Not long after the initial sale, Meskis says, she learned that the former owner and noteholder was trying to sell the note at a discount, so she took out an SBA loan to pay it off. "I've had several SBA loans over time. They're piles and piles of paperwork. It's just agony, but I'm a believer," she adds.

■ ■ ■ ■ ■ ■ ■ ■ ■

Entrepreneurial Trade-Off

Small-business owners admit they make sacrifices in exchange for their entrepreneurial life, according to a May 2007 American Express OPEN Small Business Monitor (*http://home3.americanexpress.com/corp/pc/2007/monitor.asp*).[3] Those sacrifices include:

- Family-related: 52 percent.
- Friends: 42 percent.
- Personal finances: 36 percent.
- Health: 35 percent.
- Personal life: 73 percent (males), 65 percent (females).

■ ■ ■ ■ ■ ■ ■ ■ ■

Weighing the Sacrifice

Successful entrepreneurs must make sacrifices, too. Holstein's company didn't even have $1,000 in sales in its first six months!

Dubroff didn't take a paycheck from his fledgling company for three months so he could pay severance to two people he was forced to lay off.

Jon Nordmark went nine months without a salary. He's founder and CEO of the now wildly successful eBags.com (*www.ebags.com*), the largest online purveyor of bags, as in luggage, handbags, and other bags. When Nordmark launched his business, however, it was definitely a different story. In 1997, while working as senior marketing director of luggage giant Samsonite Corporation, he recognized the potential of the then-new Internet as a sales delivery channel. But he couldn't convince his employer of it, so he quit his job to exploit the potential himself. He had found his niche.

It took Nordmark a year to find his four other co-founders—three of them from Samsonite, including an ex-president of the company. They all put in start-up cash. But, says Nordmark, he was the worst off financially because he didn't have anything to fall back on. "I got in pretty serious trouble. I think I borrowed $60,000 on my credit cards; I had a second mortgage on my house for $60,000; I went through most of my 401(k) retirement savings plan, and my savings were down to nothing. I had two months left that I could pay my mortgage."

"There were some really scary moments in the beginning," he recalls. "I remember lying in bed one night looking at the ceiling and the dog lying on my bed with me, and I was really worried that I would lose my house and everything."

Even after venture capital giant Benchmark Capital came in with solid seed money, Nordmark and his fellow execs took only modest salaries—$40,000 each—for the next six months until they received a second round of funding. Nordmark and his co-founders then upped their salaries to $80,000, still not much compared with their counterparts at other dotcom companies. "If we had known in the beginning how hard this was going to be, I don't know whether any of us would have done it," adds Nordmark.

Sam Hishmeh went without a paycheck for nearly two years as he struggled to build a tiny failing Domino's Pizza franchise he had purchased. "I had nothing to fall back on. I had to be successful," says the Jordanian immigrant, today a highly successful owner of 15 Domino's Pizza franchise locations in Southern California. As president and CEO of Hishmeh Enterprises, a Ventura, California-based company with about 400 employees, he also co-owns two Medicine Shop pharmacies.

"I was 21 when I started, and for a couple of years I had to work day and night with no pay. I worked for free, so I had no payroll expenses," says Hishmeh. "I was driver, manager, pizza maker, and the marketing guy, too. You have to sacrifice. There is no free ride, and it's not easy. If it is too easy, hardly ever is there a good outcome."

His advice to those entrepreneurs looking for success: Plan to work 100 hours a week the first couple years. "You can't be afraid of that because that's the price you have to pay, and you have to pay it up-front."

Are you willing as an entrepreneur to make the necessary financial sacrifices to build *your* company? That's a question you must answer honestly.

When the Going Gets Tough

Can you stomach tough employee decisions, too? Your small business is, after all, a business and must be run as such. If an economic downturn necessitates layoffs, that's what has to be done. Or, if you make what in retrospect is a poor hiring decision, you must be able to take the steps necessary to correct it. The survival of your business often is at stake.

From the Trenches

As a neophyte small-business owner, I learned a few lessons in making decisions. I was overly optimistic about what people could learn and accomplish, and the reality was like a bucket of cold water. When we laid off our general manager and four people in our advertising sales team in mid-2001, it was very painful. I remember a long half-hour drive to Ventura from Santa Barbara where I had to tell two people their time was up. I knew that one of them would have a difficult time finding a new job, but there was no real alternative for us. It made me feel better in a way that I was not benefitting financially from these cuts—I was going without salary for three months in order to cover some of the severance costs and to catch up on the bills.

But then my own credit card bills started to grow exponentially and I was getting a bit scared. By the time my salary resumed in the fall of 2001, I had learned a very hard lesson about what it takes to succeed in business.

You as a small-business owner must be really persistent and not give up, says Nordmark. "There's never any silver bullet because in so many things, something can always go wrong. You have to know things are going to go wrong, and you have to be OK with that and keep going."

Location Times Three

We've all heard it, but alas it's a truism. Location counts; location pays; location means success or failure.

If you're thinking about moving your existing small business, launching a retail store, planning a wholesale business, or even

opening a manufacturing facility in a certain location, some absolute musts, according to SCORE's small-business consultant
Lehman, are:

- Thoroughly check out the location.
- Find out what other businesses are in the vicinity.
- Find out who are your potential customers in the
  area if applicable.

"My cliché, no matter the business, is, 'Who is my customer
and how do I get them in my store?'" says Lehman. "Before you
open a store, you almost have to stand in front of the location and
see who is passing by. Ask yourself, 'Does that look my customer?'
Look at the other stores in the neighborhood. If you're the only
fashion store in a 2-square-mile area, ask yourself, 'Why am I so
smart to open a fashion store?' It's not always good to be the only
one around. Maybe there is a good reason."

■■■■■■■■■■

Do Your Homework Up-Front

Solid sources of information on your competition, customers,
and location include:

- Chambers of commerce.
- Better Business Bureau.
- Neighborhood businesses and industry.

■■■■■■■■■■

Do your research ahead of time, Lehman emphasizes. Check
out your state's Secretary of State's office, the Better Business
Bureau in the area, and more, to determine the community's income level and interests. Sit and talk to people in the community,
and, if possible, get a survey of what's going on. Is your product or
service a good fit with the lifestyle of the location? Can the people
afford your goods or services? Would they even want them? "If you
have a location already selected, talk to the guy next door about
the customers that he gets," says Lehman.

Cableorganizer.com's Holstein learned that lesson the hard way. After his business outgrew his garage he scouted what he thought was the perfect storefront location in a strip mall at the right rental price. Unfortunately, the move turned into a costly mistake partly because his store's next-door neighbor was a reading room that didn't provide many walk-in customers looking for cable-organizing products.

If you're looking to locate a factory, says Lehman, you'll need to ask all of the previous questions, plus a few more:

- Are enough people in town willing to work in my factory?
- Will those people work for the wages I'm willing to pay?
- Is there a ready workforce that's already trained?
- Is there a trainable workforce or are their skill levels too low to understand any training?
- Has there ever been a factory nearby? If so, why did it fail?

Check out the history of the region. Just as with a retail location, if you're the only game in town, be sure it's because no one has thought of your plan before and not because someone else made the same mistake you're about to make.

The Financial Equation

Dreams, ideas, and plans are great, but you had better know how your business will make money before you launch or relaunch. As elementary as that sounds, too many small business owners don't have a clue.

"If you can't explain to your 75-year-old mother or grandmother how your company is going to make money, it won't," says Jerry Shereshewsky, world-renowned marketing guru extraordinaire and all-around business genius. He's also the CEO of startup

Grandparents.com (*www.grandparents.com*) and former Yahoo! Ambassador Plenipotentiary to Madison Avenue (seriously!), and has been involved in the creation and marketing of a number of successful products including Gevalia coffee and Mello-Yello soft drink. In other words, Shereshewsky knows the ups and downs and ins and outs of business.

Recognize, too, that it takes cash to implement your business. You need financial backing to give your small business a chance at success. And you had better have a Plan B for backup in case things don't go your way. Remember eBags' Nordmark? In his company's dismal early months, his Plan B was the option of moving in with his mom or sister if the business failed. Once he had that plan, though, he says, he calmly went about making his company succeed, and it did.

■ ■ ■ ■ ■ ■ ■ ■ ■

Financial straightjackets do not lead to financial discipline.

—Don Peppers and Martha Rogers, authors of *Rules to Break & Laws to Follow: How Your Business Can Beat* the *Crisis of Short-Termism* (Wiley, 2008)

■ ■ ■ ■ ■ ■ ■ ■ ■

Sources of cash

Your options for cash to fund the business include self-funding, where you put up the money and take all the risk; equity capital, in which people or groups provide cash in exchange for a share of ownership in the business—generally venture capitalists or angel (private, high net worth) investors; and debt capital, in which a business borrows funds to be repaid with interest over a specified length of time.

What works best for you and your business depends on many factors, including whether you want full ownership of a business and your individual situation. It's not as difficult to find money as you might think, though. Tons of options are available if you know where to look.

Family, friends, and beyond

Talk with friends, family, and business associates and acquaintances. You'll be surprised by what a little networking turns up. That's how I found the equity capital to launch the *Pacific Coast Business Times*. That's how Meskis came up with part of the cash she used to buy the Tattered Cover.

Many retirees or ordinary people with average or above-average incomes may be "closet" angel investors willing to ante up cash for the right company with the right plans and a bright future. Nordmark garnered the first funding for eBags from former business associates, including an ex-president of the company who joined him as a co-founder. Even Craigslist (*www.craigslist.com*) and your local newspaper classifieds often have "Money Available" listings. A word of caution, however: Thoroughly check out any potential source of funding. Look for complaints filed against the individual or company, and get and talk with references. Talk to your local Secretary of State's office, too, and check with the local and national Better Business Bureau (*www.bbb.org*), various business and licensing organizations, and even check the local newspaper and industry publications for commentary and news related to that individual and/or company.

Venture capital

If your grandiose plans for your business's future are realistic, serious venture capitalists may be interested in your business. Of course, in exchange for their capital, they look for a high return on their investment, and you'll generally have to forsake some control. VCs also have the last call on the company's assets in the event the business fails. Don't overlook the additional fact that, if people invest in your company, you owe them the opportunity to get out in the form of a sale of their assets or the company in some way, says Nordmark.

A small business also may be able to secure capital from lenders such as banks, although many banks won't even consider talking with tiny entrepreneurial ventures that have no equity cushion as collateral. A bit of advice: If you're looking for this kind of funding, consider talking to small, niche business banks in your area. Often they're more willing to gamble on the community.

Don't overlook organizations such as the SBA, either. After all, loaning to small businesses is their business (*www.sba.gov*).

Charge-cards option

Although it's generally not advisable from a position of sound fiscal responsibility, many entrepreneurs turn to their charge cards for initial funding. It's risky, but so is that freefall without a parachute known as launching a small business.

As Dubroff indicated earlier, making up a cash shortfall in your business with the help of your personal charge card can get a tad too convenient and very scary. Your business, after all, likely works in terms of tens of thousands or even millions of dollars—not exactly the kind of account-due balance most of us like to carry on a regular basis.

Personal finances

If you're launching a new business or re-launching to energize your existing one, you will need to shore up your personal finances and likely garner outside funding. You will need reserves that can replace your salary as well as at least partly fund the company in an emergency. That's how Holstein prepared before launching CableOrganizer.com.

When Dubroff launched the *Pacific Coast Business Times*, his parents offered to invest in it. But he declined their offer. "I told my parents to hang on to their cash. But when the 2001 recession hit, I asked them to step up and they did. I matched their investment—giving our sagging bank balance a big boost."

Flexibility and Your Gut

If you're seldom flexible in your ideas, approaches, actions, and life, owning a small business probably isn't the best career move. Small-business success, after all, relies a great deal on the businesses and its owner/operator's ability to be flexible and react quickly to unexpected change. In that same May 2007 American Express OPEN Small Business Monitor, more than one-third of business owners surveyed named flexibility as the most essential aspect of being an entrepreneur.[3]

Your gut doesn't lie

Remember how when you were a kid and did something wrong or were about to do something you knew you better not, you would get that queasy feeling in your gut? You'll get that feeling as a small-business owner, too, when things aren't going right or are about to go terribly wrong. Learn to pay attention to that sinking feeling. As unscientific as it sounds, your gut *sometimes* can be a good indicator to help you make good decisions.

■ ■ ■ ■ ■ ■ ■ ■ ■ ■

With the leap to entrepreneurship, you can regularly expect to feel as if you just jumped out of an airplane without a parachute. But don't panic. Learn to handle the situation instead.

■ ■ ■ ■ ■ ■ ■ ■ ■

Of course, when you first make the leap to entrepreneurship, you'll regularly feel as if you just jumped out of an airplane without a parachute. In many respects you have already, especially if you've been a professional in the workforce. After all, you're leaving behind a large organization with plenty of machinery built up to cushion that company—and in some cases, you—from a hard crash. Established companies have human resource procedures to fend off lawsuits, credit lines to make up immediate cash shortfalls, information technology (IT) staff to handle computer and other system problems, and legal departments to take care of litigious threats.

As an entrepreneur, these first pangs of sheer panic come from the fact that you are free-falling into the unknown. Don't despair, however. These moments of panic are fully justified. Recognize them and pay attention to them. They will help you learn how to handle situations and put together your own strategic team/coping mechanism. As a small-business owner:

- You WILL make bad hires and get that queasy feeling in your stomach when the company is stuck in neutral because a key employee lacks commitment or skill or perhaps both.

- You WILL have to deal with high-maintenance customers who will waste your time and make you feel as if you can't succeed—until you find a way to move on to new sales.

- You WILL bump up against the limits of a poorly designed computer or phone system or a clunky Website that's hindering your attempts to get information to customers and build your business.

The feeling in the pit of your stomach will evolve, however. At first it will be sheer terror—somebody just quit and you're headed out of town on a trip and there is no one to answer the phones for a week. Eventually the gut feeling will evolve into a wake-up call every time something in the company reaches a point that stresses and strains your business's people and equipment. To handle that internal alarm, a small-business owner must develop a bank of resources: a good HR consultant, IT help, legal advisor/advisors, and perhaps a trusted office manager who can help you navigate these issues and problems.

As long as you own your business, the empty feeling is only a phone call or e-mail away. But you will learn to anticipate and cope. Remember: if you don't pay attention to that empty feeling in the pit of your stomach and make the efforts to resolve the problem, no matter how minor in the beginning, it likely can become a disaster. Picture what might or might not have happened to corporate tragedies such as Enron or WorldCom if their senior management had listened to the women in those companies who experienced that empty feeling and sent word up the line that something wasn't right, only to be smacked down.

Their Weaknesses Can Be Your Strengths

Plenty of people will discourage your small-business aspirations. Among their rationales:

- There's too much competition.
- The economy is in terrible shape.
- You can't win.
- You don't have the experience.

Instead of agreeing with those naysayers, look closely at the competition. What are their weaknesses? Those can become your strengths. That's easy to say, but it happens to be true, too. When Holstein started CableOrganizer.com, it wasn't that no one sold cable organizers. It was just that no one else did a good job of helping potential customers understand cable-management products and recognize the need for them, says Holstein.

When Meskis took over the Tattered Cover, it wasn't that no one else sold books in Denver. It was that she did it better. Ditto with Imperial Headwear and hats, the *Pacific Coast Business Times* and business news, and Kinko's and copies.

When Janet Goldberg, a former schoolteacher in Southern California, and her husband, Joel, launched Bali Hai Travel Agency (today GreatHawaiiVacations.com—*www.greathawaiivacations.com*), it wasn't that there were no travel agencies offering vacations to Hawaii. The difference, Goldberg says, was that, "We know our product; we know Hawaii. We offer great customer service. That's what sets us apart."

Smaller companies learn a lot of tough lessons at the hands of Goliath-sized competitors, says entrepreneur Harvey Mackay. "The big guys are always happy to teach them, too. Get on the Internet every day and follow how investment and trade media are sizing them up. Success and dominance always breed complacency. What are the chinks in the big guys' armour? There is critical buzz about every competitor, and it never hurts to know it. Focus your energy on what meaningful things you (as a small-business owner) can do (to compete)," says Mackay.

■ ■ ■ ■ ■ ■ ■ ■ ■

SBA Self-Assessment: Are You Ready to Start a Business?

The U.S. Small Business Administration offers a free interactive self-assessment tool on its Website (www.sba.gov) *to help you determine your readiness to start a business. You'll find help with and answers to many of these questions in this book. Here's a sample of some of the questions:*

General:

- *Do you have enough confidence in yourself and your abilities to sustain yourself in business if or when things get tough?*
- *Do you like to make your own decisions?*
- *Are you prepared, if needed, to temporarily lower your standard of living until your business is firmly established?*
- *Do others turn to you for help in making decisions?*
- *Are you willing to commit long hours to make your business work?*
- *Would others consider you a team player?*

Your skills, experience, and training:

- *Do you have a business plan for the business you are planning to start?*
- *Do you know and understand the components of a business plan?*
- *Do you know if your business will require a special license or permit and how to obtain it?*

- Do you know where to find demographic data and information about your customers?
- Do you know how to compute a financial break-even point for your business?
- Do you know how to compute the startup costs for your business?
- Do you know how to prepare and/or interpret a balance sheet, income statement, and cash-flow statement?
- Are you sure your planned business fits a specific market need?
- Do you know your target market?
- Do you understand tax requirements associated with your business?
- Do you know how to prepare a marketing strategy for your business?
- Do you know how to learn about your business competitors?
- Do you understand marketing trends in your business industry?
- Do you know where to obtain information about regulations and compliance requirements that impact your business?
- Do you feel comfortable using a computer or other technology to improve business operations?
- Do you have a payroll process planned for your business?
- Do you have a customer service strategy in mind or in place?

Source: SBA.[4]

Your Ammunition

Some essentials to remember from this chapter include:

- Perseverance goes with the territory of owning a small business.

■ Working from home a bit on the side, or saying you're in business for yourself, isn't the same as becoming an owner/operator of a small business, making the decision to start a company, finding your niche, laying out your plans, and carrying through with them.

■ If you're not flexible in your ideas, approaches, actions, and life, owning a small-business likely isn't for you, because small business success requires flexibility and quick reaction to change.

■ Be prepared for the inevitable panic over circumstances and events. You will survive if you take those panics in stride.

■ Instead of fearing your competition, analyze it, determine what it does right and wrong, and then figure out what you can do to surpass it.

PART
II

THE PLAN OF ATTACK

CHAPTER
3

EMPOWERING YOUR EMPLOYEES

The person who is everywhere is nowhere.
—Harvey Mackay, author, speaker, entrepreneur

You can't do it ALL yourself. Too many small-business owners/operators try, and they fail. A big part of long-term success in the realm of small business involves finding good employees, knowing how to train them properly, providing them with the tools they need, and empowering them to win. All of this occurs within the context of operating a lean organization with the help of technology, trust, and intensity.

Sounds like a fairy tale, right? Wrong! It's reality, plain and simple. Hire the right employees, treat them right, and then throw away the time clock, because you will get more from your team than if you micromanage them and keep track of every minute.

The right employees are everything, says Tattered Cover's Meskis. "You can't do it alone. I'm the face of the business, but they're the everyday connection to the customer. The people with whom I work are the bedrock of the business. Absolutely."

"A company is a group of people," says eBags's Nordmark. "It's not one entrepreneur."

Your team is paramount, agrees Vera Bradley's Miller. And, she adds, "Any company that's successful probably does a great job of training their employees."

Let's look more closely.

The Setting

"There's a war for talent going on," says John A. Challenger, CEO of Chicago-based international outplacement firm Challenger, Gray & Christmas. "It's going to get tougher and tougher as the Baby Boomers start to retire. Many think labor shortages are on the horizon, so finding the most talented people is going to be crucial to the most successful businesses in the future."

Challenger should know. For decades, he and the firm founded by his father in the 1960s have tracked hirings, firings, and workplace trends across the spectrum. The younger Challenger also is among the most-quoted experts in the industry.

Small is big yet again

With a limited employee pool and a pitched battle for talent, you as a small-business owner may think there's no way you can compete with the Big Boxes for workers. But once again, small is big. Shift your attitude into the positive column, because you can compete and attract the very best talent in the marketplace.

Many top-notch people prefer the freedom of a small business run right, where they feel they can "make a difference," as opposed to the limitations of a corporate flow chart where they are just another FTE (full-time equivalent)—corporate jargon for a full-time employee. In fact, you may have started out in business as one of those FTEs. If so, think back to what you didn't like about the company and how you were or weren't treated. Did you leave that company, perhaps in part, to fulfill personal ambitions because you felt unwanted, underappreciated, ignored, or stifled? Don't lose sight of the importance of employee morale within your own company, and create your work environment, corporate culture, and employee policies accordingly.

Though compensation is the most important element of job satisfaction across the board for employees no matter the size of the company, employees of small organizations place less importance on what they earn than their counterparts at larger companies, according to the 2007 Job Satisfaction survey from the Alexandria, Virginia–based Society of Human Resource Management industry organization (*www.shrm.org*).[1] The survey showed that job satisfaction for employees at small companies (99 employees or fewer) depends on a number of things, including, in descending order of importance:

- Compensation/pay.
- Job security.
- Communication between employees and senior management.
- Autonomy and independence.
- Management recognition of employee job performance.
- Relationship with immediate supervisor.
- Benefits.
- Overall corporate culture/relationship with coworkers (tie).
- Career development opportunities.
- Organization's commitment to professional development.
- Job-specific training.
- Career advancement opportunities.
- Paid training and tuition reimbursement programs.

Employees of medium-sized companies with 100 to 499 employees rated aspects of job satisfaction slightly differently. Also in descending order of importance, they include:

- Compensation/pay.
- Benefits.
- Job security.
- Communication between employees and senior management.
- Relationship with immediate supervisor.
- Management recognition of employee job performance.
- Overall corporate culture.
- Autonomy and independence.
- Relationship with coworkers.
- Career development opportunities.
- Organization's commitment to professional development.
- Job-specific training.
- Paid training and tuition reimbursement programs.
- Career advancement opportunities.

■ ■ ■ ■ ■ ■ ■ ■ ■

Very Important Aspects of Job Satisfaction

Here's a breakdown of how employees of companies of any size ranked the following as "very important" to their job satisfaction, according to the 2007 Job Satisfaction survey from the Society of Human Resource Management:

- Compensation/pay: 59 percent.
- Benefits: 59 percent.
- Job security: 53 percent.
- Flexibility to balance life and work issues: 52 percent.
- Communication between employees and senior management: 51 percent.
- Feeling safe in the work environment: 50 percent.

- Management recognition of employee job performance: 49 percent.
- Relationship with immediate supervisor: 48 percent.
- Autonomy and independence: 44 percent.
- Opportunities to use skills/abilities: 44 percent.
- The work itself: 41 percent.
- Meaningfulness of job: 37 percent.
- Overall corporate culture: 36 percent.
- Career development opportunities: 35 percent.
- Variety of work: 34 percent.
- Relationship with co-workers: 34 percent.
- Contribution of work to organization's business goals: 32 percent.
- Paid training and tuition reimbursement programs: 31 percent.
- Organization's commitment to (their) professional development: 31 percent.
- Career advancement opportunities: 28 percent.
- Job-specific training: 27 percent.
- Networking: 18 percent.[2]

Source: SHRM 2007 Job Satisfaction Survey Report.

■ ■ ■ ■ ■ ■ ■

Your Very Own Orchestra

You as owner are conductor of the chamber orchestra that is your business. You lead your team of people, who generally are specialists in what they do, by gently cueing them to react correctly. What you do as conductor and how you treat your employees provide clues to how your business will operate. Cue/treat your employees poorly, and your business will do poorly long term. Cue/treat them right, and they'll treat you and your business well, too.

As a small-business owner, you need a good grounding in personnel management. That means management expertise and training to help you understand how to behave in ways to motivate and build trust. If you don't already have that training and expertise, get it. Plenty of organizations, including colleges and universities as well as companies online and off, offer classes.

"You have to know how to hire people, too, and not just how to get the most out of your employees," says Sheryl Garrett, founder of the Garrett Planning Network, an international network of nearly 300 fee-only financial planners. That means knowing the right questions to ask potential job candidates. In the early years of her company, Garrett says she didn't have the necessary skills and made some poor hires as a result. Her solution: "Outsourcing HR would have been an option or if I could have gone to a one-day workshop on asking the right questions."

If you need motivation to get the training, keep in mind that your employees' satisfaction is key to your success. If people eagerly come to work every day, your chances for success go up exponentially. "As small businesses sometimes we don't have the cash to pamper our employees. But our employees are our lifeblood," adds Garrett.

Finding Talent

One of the biggest human-resources mistakes that small businesses make is to not seek out great talent, adds Challenger. Many small businesses don't even have a designated human resources department, which could be as small as one qualified person with the talent and job description to be responsible for the hiring, coordination of processes, training, integration, and development of talent. "Too many small businesses recruit and hire without really thinking through who they want or without being patient enough to find the right person simply because they don't have the people in place to do it. They just kind of get the job filled," says Challenger. "Once they have someone on board, they often throw that person into a job and adopt a sink-or-swim method. That method is very expensive if a large percentage of the people you hire sink."

They sink because they move into a job, aren't really aware of their responsibilities or where they fit in the organization, don't receive adequate training or guidance, and then basically aren't very adept at figuring it all out on their own and integrating themselves into your organization, he adds.

HR Is Important

Such hit-or-miss hiring doesn't have to be the norm, Challenger says, if small-business owners consciously decide to recognize that HR processes and procedures are important and ongoing. HR isn't about simply hiring one person and moving on.

Don't buy into the line that "it's too expensive" to make the human resources commitment, either. You can't afford not to! A small business, after all, doesn't have the luxury of costly personnel mistakes. Paying attention to HR doesn't necessarily mean a burdensome cash outlay, either. The commitment could be as simple as taking the time as business owner to work on your company's organization and development. You can designate one specific person to handle the HR function or even decide to do it yourself. But keep in mind that the job of hiring someone should include more than just getting them to sign up to work for you. Hiring done right means training and integrating them into your organization, too. That's what's known in HR lingo as on-boarding, says Challenger. That includes working to help your employees resolve workplace issues, evaluating their performance based on quantitative measures, and then knocking out the bad hires quickly rather than allowing them to fester and foster ill will.

Even with HR people on staff or outsourced, you as the owner/operator absolutely need people skills for your business to survive and thrive. Your employees need to know and feel that you are trustworthy and fair, and you need to know how to motivate your employees to get the job, whatever it is, done right. That means if you don't already have those attributes, learn how to develop them. Take a class from a local community college, work with a coach (more on that in Chapter 7), or simply recognize your weakness and work at correcting it. Keep in mind, too, independent bookstore owner Meskis's lesson in perseverance, and heed her advice: "If you come up short in one area, that's not cause to panic. It is cause to correct the problem."

Outside Help

Plenty of low-cost options are available to help you get a handle on your company's HR operations or lack thereof. That includes self-employed HR consultants, or online or local companies you can hire on either a project basis or ongoing. To find potential candidates, talk to other small-business owners in your area and network through local organizations. Find out who handles their HR. You also can check local classified ads and, of course, Craigslist.org. If you do opt for an outside individual or organization, as with any contractor, get references and thoroughly check them out. Talk to your local Better Business Bureau, online at BBB.org, and with your Secretary of State's Office.

Avoiding paralysis

The last thing your small business can afford is personal paralysis when it comes to tapping top talent, training it, and integrating it into your business.

When I suddenly found myself ready to hire key people for the *Pacific Coast Business Times*, I froze. As a reporter and editor, I'd interviewed thousands of people for thousands of stories in my professional life and given dozens of speeches in front of strangers, but suddenly I was paralyzed as to where to even begin to look for potential hires. Similar to many small businesses that don't have or can't afford an HR department, I was stymied. Craigslist hadn't really taken off yet, and I hadn't spent enough time pondering sources of possible talent.

Eventually, though, I wised up to what proved to be a free goldmine of talent: the local college campus. That's a great option, especially if you're a start up with minimal cash. You can advertise jobs on bulletin boards near specific departments relating to your needs as well as in campus newspapers. In our case, I posted jobs on the bulletin board outside the campus newspaper offices at the University of California-Santa Barbara. From only one no-cost posting, I picked up a highly qualified part-time real estate editor, a lead photographer, a news editor, and a copyeditor.

Current employees, family, friends

People enjoy having friends at work. The workplace is, after all, a community. Several of my hires already were friends, familiar with each other, and accustomed to being together. The workplace was a natural extension of their relationship, and a successful one, too.

Current employees who like their job, do well, and enjoy working for you are a good source of other potential employees, agrees Challenger. "Having a friend at work is a very important part of finding people who come in and stay for the long term and do good work and take pride in the company."

When the *Pacific Coast Business Times* needed an accountant, our banker actually suggested that her husband, Fran Burrus, who was retiring from his full-time accounting position, might be willing to help us part-time. It made me a little nervous to think about hiring our banker's husband as our accountant; he was a minor legend in Santa Barbara who had an impeccable reputation and was known as somebody who could fix things. Bingo! He remained our accountant for the next four years. Never rule out an option until you thoroughly check it out.

Many small businesses also hire family members. Not only is the family a source of talent, but usually has a strong degree of commitment, adds Challenger. If you do hire family members, it's essential to set high performance standards for them and make sure they're met.

The job bank option

Challenger also suggests that small businesses advertise for top talent on local or industry-specific job banks. If, for example, you're looking for an accountant, consider the local, national, or regional CPA (certified public accountant) society's job board. For human resources, the Society of Human Resource Management or its local association can be a good source. Even a local community college, your university alumni office, a local church or synagogue, or people with whom you meet and talk in the community can net successful job candidates. "In a really small business serving a very local market, try posting an ad on the bulletin boards at the grocery store, too," says Challenger.

If the job posting at UC-Santa Barbara hadn't worked, I could have tried the Society of American Business Editors and Writers (*www.sabew.org*).

Online up close

Beyond online options to advertise for potential hires, don't overlook online, virtual sources to meet your HR needs, either. Companies such as Robert Half International (*www.RHI.net*), Administaff (*www.administaff.com*), SurePayroll (*www.surepayroll.com*), or smaller, local firms can be an excellent source of help and hires to tap at reasonable prices. That goes for whether you need payroll administration, benefit coordination, training, and more. HR giants such as Watson Wyatt Worldwide (*www.watsonwyatt.com*)—even though it deals with Fortune 500 companies and the like—can be excellent sources of benchmarks and trends, whether pertaining to compensation and benefits, or workplace and employee issues and concerns. Most generally have free e-mail newsletters, white papers, and research reports that they regularly send out automatically. All it takes is a simple sign-up on your part—no cash and no commitment. Local, regional, and national industry organizations generally do the same thing, so take advantage of what they have to offer. It's free, it's easy, and sources such as these offer great tips on whatever topic you're interested in. Even if you pick up only one nugget out of several newsletters, it's worth it in the long run.

■ ■ ■ ■ ■ ■ ■ ■

Finding the Right Employees

Outplacement expert John Challenger suggests paying attention to solid, old-school traits when considering potential employees:

- Do they have integrity and honesty? Do they verbalize it?
- Are they hardworking?
- Are they committed to what they do so they stay in the job? Does that reflect in their work history?
- Do they fit with the people in your workplace? Will people get along with them, and will they be a part of the company community?

■ ■ ■ ■ ■ ■ ■ ■ ■

Empowering to Win

Long-term success is no solo trek. You can't do it alone and without the help and support of employees. You foster greatness in your employees by empowering them. That means providing support and encouragement, training and guidance, and creating an environment in which they want you and the business to succeed.

Part of empowering your people is to always have fresh ideas, says Denver's Mayor Hickenlooper. "I had a writing professor in college who said, 'Everything has been said, but not everything has been said superbly. And even if it has, everything must be said freshly again and again.' Your employees become a great way of finding fresh ways to say things and a source for innovative ideas. We got a lot of our best ideas from our employees," he adds.

Three of four small employers specifically and directly encourage their employees to suggest ideas for new products and services or better ways to produce and distribute them, according to an NFIB 411 Small Business Facts poll on Innovation.[3] To encourage that innovation, 51 percent of those employers offer bonuses or special recognition to those employees who make suggestions used to increase business productivity or sales, poll numbers show.

Give the right cues

No matter how large or small your business, or whether you have a handful or hundreds of employees, you as the conductor of the chamber orchestra can cue those employees to do great things. In the long term, if you use your influence in the right way, your employees will listen and follow your orders. But if you simply wave your baton wildly, the "musicians" will stray and your product or service will suffer. Remember: It's not about forcing your employees into submission or squeezing every last ounce of work from them. It's about creating a workplace, a framework, and an attitude so that your employees WANT to do their very best to make the business succeed.

■ ■ ■ ■ ■ ■ ■ ■

Great leaders create a circle of success for all around them, and in doing so gain their trust, support, and loyalty.
—John M. McKee (*www.businesssuccesscoach.net*), business and career success coach, and author

■ ■ ■ ■ ■ ■ ■ ■

Great leaders, after all, help others to succeed. They mentor, lead by example, train, and assist others to be better at what they do. "They create a circle of success for all around them, and in doing so gain their trust, support, and loyalty," says John M. McKee (*www.businesssuccesscoach.net*), one of America's leading business and career success coaches, and author of *Career Wisdom: 101 Proven Strategies to Ensure Workplace Success* (Wheatmark, 2007) and *21 Ways Women in Management Shoot Themselves in the Foot* (Wheatmark, 2006).

Lead by example, says Alice H. Magos, who is the Ask Alice columnist for Business Owner's Toolkit (*www.toolkit.com*). Toolkit is a free information and advice Website from CCH Incorporated, a Wolters Kluwer business and a leading tax and legal information provider to professionals since 1913. "The speed of the boss will be the speed of his (or her) employees," says Magos.

"A good manager is always willing to get into the trenches with the troops. Loyalty and respect are built this way," Magos advises business owners. "If your car rental agency is oversold this weekend, or you sold a lemon or delivered the wrong couch, get out there and take the abuse from the disgruntled customers yourself. They'll be less disgruntled if they see you personally trying to solve the problem. Set a professional example for your people. Show up earlier, stay later, and never, ever complain!! That is LEADER-SHIP. It's what good bosses do."[4]

Great leaders are also great listeners, says McKee. They not only listen to but actually hear and care about the information being imparted to them. Another hallmark of a great leader, adds McKee, is understanding the difference between power and force. Forcing an employee to do something may create a short-term victory, but it often results in employee resentment and long-term negative results, says McKee. Your power as a business leader is enhanced, however, when you help employees reach their own conclusions—in part by constructively exposing them to all points of view. This approach, although time-consuming, ultimately leads to more lasting results with employees who are more engaged and more productive, McKee says.

A big part of any restaurant's efforts at success is paying attention to your cash flow down to the smallest detail, says Hickenlooper. "The more you do that, the more your employees do that. And that's part of empowering your employees, to make sure that they have responsibility for the finance of the enterprise, and that they also have the incentive to be responsible. If they can find a cheaper way to do something, there should be some benefit to them," he adds.

Corporate Culture

You create the internal environment or corporate culture of your company. What you do and what you expect from your employees in terms of their appearance, attitude, commitment, and behavior toward you, other employees, and your customers—the lifeblood of your business—sets the tone. If you're short-tempered and disrespectful with employees and/or customers, you end up with disgruntled, disrespectful employees. If you short-change your employees in terms of respect, compensation, appreciation, and more, they'll shortchange you, too, and jump ship without a second thought.

A positive corporate culture can be as simple as going out of your way to accommodate the legitimate needs of your employees, recognizing and rewarding their ideas and efforts, and making sure they know their importance to the organization. It's a simple statement. Of course, implementing it may not be.

GreatHawaiiVacations.com's Janet Goldberg points to her company's positive approach to business and its employees—right now the company has about 20—as an essential part of her small business's ongoing success, especially in tougher economic times. "I think the attitude of our management team giving it their all permeates throughout the office," she says.

"Right now times are extremely challenging, yet I feel like I have such a great team," says Goldberg, whose company has very low turnover. "Our employees are fabulous; our management team is fabulous. Everyone is giving it their all with a good attitude, being proactive, and thinking way outside the box. We have a win-win attitude toward our employees—we don't want us to be winners and them to be losers, or vice versa. We compensate them very well; we always try to help them further their skills, and we help them provide a good income for themselves. We care about the quality of their lives, and we expect a lot from them because we want our clients to get the best."

Happy, productive employees help to generate success, and it's no coincidence that some of the most successful companies end up on the Best Places to Work lists year in and year out. Remember Paul Orfalea, who turned one tiny copy service into giant Kinko's and made tens of millions of dollars in the process? Orfalea garnered honors for his philosophies and how he treated his employees, too. *Fortune* magazine named Kinko's one of the 100 Best Companies to Work in America in 1999, 2000, and 2001, and *Working Mother* listed it among its Best Companies for Working Mothers in 2001.[5] Even though he sold Kinko's, Orfalea has continued to work with the government and businesses in support of creating family-friendly work/life environments. He empowered his employees through this philosophy even when his small business was only one tiny store.

"As Kinko's grew, our biggest challenge was moving from a culture of *things* to a culture of *people*," says Orfalea. "A 200-square-foot store could be operated by one or two people, but there were a lot of machines and systems to master. Customers were important, of course, but our services were so novel that even customers were more interested in the *things* that defined Kinko's. Before long, though, Kinko's stores were over 5,000 square feet, serving more than 1,000 customers per day, and the store manager was responsible for dozens of coworkers. By then the coworkers, not the machines or procedures, defined the company," he adds.

Successfully moving from a culture of things to one of people requires the following essentials, says Orfalea:

1. **Declare your values:** "At Kinko's we heavily publicized the company philosophy and commitment to communication. These documents expressed our expectations of one another, helped coworkers find meaning in their work, and provided a sort of constitution we could turn to when facing difficult decisions. Two of the competencies of leadership, as detailed by USC Professor Warren Bennis, are managing meaning and managing trust. A clear declaration of values serves both of these needs," says Orfalea.

2. **Manage management:** "A culture of people must be a culture of empowered people," adds Orfalea, "so try to maintain a very flat organization chart. Too many levels of management obscure communication and allow people to avoid thinking for themselves. As has often been said, we manage things and lead people. A company with too many managers is treating its people like things."

3. **Celebrate coworkers.** "It sounds very cynical when I say, 'Give the glory, keep the money,'" he adds, "but it's just a funny way of saying, give the people what they want. Most people want recognition, and they deserve it. By building both recognition and opportunity into your company's value system, you can share plenty of glory *and money* with those who seek them. But no matter what, thank your co-workers loudly and often for their contributions."

CableOrganizer's Holstein has 44 employees, and listens to what each says, recognizes their successes (both with cash rewards and sometimes even little stickers!), and tries to create a safe environment where employees aren't afraid to speak up. "I strongly believe that every employee's opinion counts. We regularly solicit ideas, offer bonuses with almost every position, and as much as possible, empower employees with the belief that this is their company. The employees do know when something's wrong and they do know how to fix things," says Holstein.

In Tune With Your Employees

"You have almost a familial relationship with the people with whom you work," says Tattered Cover's Meskis, and that relationship must be nurtured.

The secret to business success lies in your personality and attitude, which affect your ability to connect to people, whether employees or customers, adds Domino's Pizza franchisee Hishmeh.

"You have to be nice, warm, sincere, and ethical. These qualities must be in place for you to have people work for you and with you. If you have them, that's half the battle. The other half is the business plan, execution, and operations."

"My biggest fear right now is to get too big to stay in close touch with my employees, to not know them well enough to maintain their loyalty," adds Hishmeh, after returning from a lunch meeting with one of his managers.

Losing touch is a common fault in many big U.S. companies, he believes, but he works hard not to fall victim to that disconnect.

"I personally take the time once a quarter to visit my stores and spend 10 minutes with each employee, learning about them and soliciting their feedback and opinion about the way we run the company," Hishmeh says. That's a tall order, considering his company has about 400 employees!

Staying connected is a top priority for Craigslist.org's Newmark, too. Craigslist has a network of more than 500 city Websites around the world that operates with only 26 employees. In his early years with the company, founder Newmark's biggest fear was that he would fail by losing touch with people—his employees and others. That's still his biggest fear in business.

"To keep from losing touch, I'm committed to doing customer service and then following through with that commitment," says Newmark.

Orfalea stayed in touch with his business outlets, too. "A friend is writing a book about the Kinko's culture and he calls the chapter about me 'The Pot Stirrer,'" says Orfalea. "And that really was my main role. I spent my whole career raising a ruckus, traveling from store to store, finding good ideas, and gossiping about them everywhere I went. I questioned everything, but here's what made that useful: We created an environment that allowed individuals to pursue answers to those questions. We really tried to decentralize control, so each store could freely experiment with new products, new services, and new methods. We had 1,000 research and development labs cleverly disguised as stores," he adds.

■ ■ ■ ■ ■ ■ ■ ■ ■

Empower Your Employees

Following are a few ways to empower your employees:

■ *Set the example of ethics, integrity, sincerity, and excellence in your business.*

■ *Stay connected with your business and your employees through regular interaction.*

■ *Solicit and listen to employee feedback.*

■ *Recognize excellence.*

■ ■ ■ ■ ■ ■ ■ ■ ■

The Brand Connection

Think about the most successful small business of which you're aware. Now consider the employees of that business. Are they surly and obnoxious or helpful, friendly, and willing to do anything—no matter how small—to help you? It's a pretty good bet that if the company has been around very long, its employees are helpful and personable and play an important role in bringing customers back again and again. Think GreatHawaiiVacations.com; think Kinko's; think those small businesses you frequent. The employees are part of that small business's brand, its public face, its public perception. (We'll talk more about brand in the next chapter.) Employee turnover is probably low. That's because, if the employees of a company are happy and believe the company for which they work appreciates and respects them and their work, they'll work harder to do a good job. They WILL make a difference.

Keep in mind, too, that your employees—current as well as former—are purveyors of your brand whether you like it or not, consciously or unconsciously; don't forget that when you're hiring or firing. The old adage "don't burn your bridges" is especially relevant to a small business.

Money isn't everything—honest! Sure, it helps, especially in today's tough economic times. But every one of us knows from our own experience or that of others what it's like to make good money, but nonetheless be unhappy at work. Such employees are always complaining, always looking for a "better" job, and will leap at an opportunity when it comes along. Their disgruntled attitude also can infect others. Odds are that their employer cuts HR corners, does the absolute minimum required for his or her employees, and seldom, if ever, has a realistic view of what's happening with the business.

Act Now for Success

This may sound a bit elementary and hokey, but happy employees make good employees. Really! Treat them right, pay them right—including raises when appropriate—and your small business becomes one big happy/successful family.

■ ■ ■ ■ ■ ■ ■ ■ ■

Tips to Happier Employees

The Better Business Bureau offers these suggestions to boost employee happiness on the job:[6]

■ Understand why people are working and commit to help them achieve their goals on the job. Develop a plan that will help them get where they want to go.

■ Empower workers to do the job you hired them to do. A work environment in which employees are constantly monitored, micromanaged, and bossed around can be stifling. Although most employees are capable of receiving empowerment, not all will seek it. The overriding motivation for all employees is to be treated with respect.

■ Keep employees informed. Share the big picture as to why they are being asked to do what they do and how their work can benefit others. Invite them to share their opinions. Allow them to actively participate in the discussions that lead to business decisions. By including them, you signal that you value their expertise and recognize that they are a valuable asset to the organization. Remember: Involvement equals commitment!

- Communicate your expectations. Let your employees know what you expect from them in terms of work ethic, quality, honesty, and job performance. Do not assume that employees somehow inherently understand what is required.

- Take care of the people who work for you. Recognize their accomplishments with frequent and sincere praise. Take time to single out employees who have gone well beyond the call of duty.

- Hire the best people for the job, give them directions and tools to do the job, and step aside. But, be sure to follow up.

- Treat employees the way you would want to be treated. Think about how you would want to be informed of changes or acknowledged for a job well done. Then do the same with your employees.

■ ■ ■ ■ ■ ■ ■ ■ ■

Employee Recognition

We all need positive reinforcement for our actions, and the workplace is no exception. Employees need to know if they're doing something correctly or not, especially if their approach, work, or ideas are exemplary. We've all heard about or observed the long-time employee who toils day in and day for the big corporation. He never hears a word of feedback unless he screws up, and then it's a memo stating that, if he messes up one more time, he's out. This scenario plays out at small businesses, too. The owner gets caught up in his or her business or life and never bothers to provide employee feedback.

Many companies have formal feedback and goal/reward procedures. That's great if your business is conducive to that. Sales incentives are a good example. If an individual generates a certain amount in sales or satisfied customers, he or she receives a certain reward—monetary or otherwise. But keep in mind that you can generate a strong positive vibe without a lot of work, time, or expense on your part. Remember Domino's franchise owner Hishmeh? He spends only 10 minutes with each employee, but that time is one on one, no interruptions.

Even a simple thank-you card can go a long way toward making an employee feel appreciated and an integral part of the organization. If you think that's too much work, take a Sunday afternoon and write up a box or two of thank-you notes, then squirrel them away for when you need them. If yours is a bigger company, consider making the handwritten thank-you card a part of the HR department's responsibilities.

That little extra when it comes to appreciation goes beyond your employees to your suppliers and vendors, too. Kids' clothing retailer Pantella singles out one vendor that always tosses a few pieces of honey candy into all the boxes they ship to her store. "It's a small expense that lets people know they really do care," she says. Incidentally, Pantella sends out thank-you notes to her customers, too.

Employee Performance and Compensation

Set formal goals and expectations for your employees, and do so in writing to provide a set of benchmarks for both you and the employee to use to measure performance. This also provides a concrete set of standards you can link to employee compensation enhancements. There's nothing worse—and possibly more morale-deflating—than working for a company that's arbitrary in its pay scales and where the boss hands out raises to his or her "buddies." A friend once worked for a small business—about 200 employees—that doled out exactly twice as much in holiday bonuses to its male employees than to its female ones. The boss rationalized that it wasn't necessary to give the females as much because their husbands supported them!

Today, that's gender discrimination. Although it's not the easiest case to prove in court, it's not the best situation for a business, regardless. To avoid all that and more, put your policies in writing and base them on sound (and legal) performance measures. The U.S. Department of Labor offers plenty of free information and guidelines on its Website (*www.dol.gov*). A good HR specialist or outsourcer should be familiar with the rules, too. (If you're considering hiring one, don't hesitate to quiz applicants on some of the main rules. If they're clueless, you might want to focus your hiring efforts elsewhere.)

Performance benchmarks will help you maintain and administer employee accountability, as well. Accountability and taking responsibility for one's actions are key to ensuring quality in your company's product or service, and in turn protecting your brand. (We'll talk more about both later in the book.)

Of course, not all employees are posters for top performers, and not all employees work out, either. When discipline is necessary, though, try to find common sense solutions to the problems. If dismissal is inevitable, don't do it until you've thoroughly checked out all the laws that may be involved and have made sure you're in compliance with *all of* them. Check with your lawyer and HR consultant if necessary, too.

When you're figuring compensation, remember that you get what you pay for. There's a reason the counter person at the local fast-food outlet may have difficulty counting the change. Don't forget Goldberg's "win-win" approach to compensating her employees, either—if she and her husband as company owners are financially successful, their employees should be financially successful, too.

Keep your salaries competitive, period. Small and medium-sized businesses reported an average 5.8 percent increase in salaries and 3.9 percent in commissions during the second quarter of this year compared with the same period a year ago, according to Administaff's Business Confidence Survey released in August. By "average," that means some salaries and commissions went up more and others less![7]

Don't short-change an employee on the way out the door, either. You wouldn't do that to a customer. Any former employee is your company's unwitting ambassador.

To Outsource or Not

Another 30 percent planned to look to their current workforce to make up the differences this year. Outsourcing is a very individual decision that each small business owner must make him- or herself. There is no right or wrong answer unless your customers are adversely affected. As a small business you cannot afford to lose customers, especially in a down economic cycle.

■ ■ ■ ■ ■ ■ ■

Even if you only have only two employees, unless you are an accounting firm—and you would think that I might fall into that category as a financial advisor, but I don't—outsource your payroll.

—Sheryl Garrett, founder The Garret Planning Network

■ ■ ■ ■ ■ ■ ■ ■

Outsourcing has a place, says market expert Rogers. "The real question is: How will it affect the experience your customers have? I do not think that outsourcing is universally bad. In some cases, people who do the same thing all the time can do it well. So if it's more cost-efficient and done well, consider it," says Rogers. "But never outsource anything just to get a job done and save money."

If you're considering outsourcing, ask yourself, too, whether you're capable of doing the process or procedure in-house. Do you have the people, processes, expertise, and technologies to do it yourself? If the answer is no, you're a candidate to outsource.

The Telecommuting/Virtual Option

Where do you work? At home, in an office, in your car, the gym, while walking the dog, all of the above, some of the above, or somewhere else entirely? Welcome to workplace 2008. We're a workplace-everywhere world, and your small business is no different. In 2006 nearly 29 million people, or about 8 percent of the estimated 149.3 million-strong U.S. labor force, telecommuted at least one day a month, according to statistics from WorldatWork (*www.worldatwork.org*), an association of HR professionals for Fortune 500 and other companies. (© 2008. Reprinted with permission from WorldatWork).[8] However, that number has grown considerably in two years. Approximately 14 percent of private-sector employees and 17 percent of federal employees now telework, according to the survey of federal and private-sector employees and IT professionals by CDW Corporation, a leading private provider of technology solutions for federal, state, and local government agencies and educational institutions.[9]

Obviously, a virtual office doesn't make sense for all businesses. If, for example, you have a very broad, very visual product line that requires people to actually see, touch, and try on or try out your products, an online storefront might not be a good idea. But consider the case of CableOrganizer. Holstein learned a costly lesson that a strip mall store actually disrupted his business, as opposed to increasing it. Online retailer eBags.com, on the other hand, has sold 6.8 million bags and all virtually.

With today's advent of small-business services facilities complete with meeting space and more, many businesses don't need the full-time expense of a storefront with the accompanying elaborate infrastructure.

By enabling your employees to work virtually, you save the infrastructure costs associated with an office and provide your employees quality of life advantages, too. But be forewarned: If employees do work virtually or telecommute, don't sweat the hours they work or the minutiae. Pay attention to the specific performance benchmarks you've set and whether the employees are meeting them or not. Chances are that virtual employees not only will meet the benchmarks, but far exceed them.

The Garrett Planning Network went virtual more than three years ago and has absolutely no plans to return to a more traditional office space. The motivation for the move wasn't cash, although it's a nice perk to the tune of $1,600-plus a month, says Sheryl Garrett. "It just seemed wasteful in terms of time and commuting. When we would get to the office, we would go into our offices and instant message each other anyway.

"We did it (went virtual) not knowing for sure if people would like it, and we more than like it," says Garrett. In fact, Garrett herself is moving her office from Shawnee Mission, Kansas, to Beaver Lake in northwestern Arkansas, and most of her employees already have moved elsewhere. "When you go virtual, you can be anywhere as long as there's an Internet and a phone. In theory, I could be in Sweden," she adds. "It's a huge perk to our employees, too, because three out of five of us have little kids at home."

Termination: Just Do It!

No one likes to fire someone, probably least of all someone who is part of a small business "family." Think of the agony I described in the last chapter when I had to let two employees go. But my business's survival depended on it. The survival of most small businesses likely depends on the ability to fire as well as hire the right people.

"As a small-business owner, the hardest decisions are to let people go," says Challenger. "But you do have to do it when they're not performing well."

To help him come to terms with the trauma of terminating an employee, especially one he knows well, Challenger says he generally ends up deciding it's the right thing for both parties. "If it's not working out for the company—the person isn't performing in their role—then it can't be working out for them, either. They need to find a job that's meaningful, that they can be good at."

"Remember, it's not the people you fire who make your life miserable, it's the people you don't fire," says Harvey Mackay, author of *We Got Fired...and It's the Best Thing that Ever Happened to Us* (Ballantine, 2004).

■ ■ ■ ■ ■ ■ ■ ■

Do you have a tough people decision on your plate? Act on it and get it over with. It will be better for all involved.

—Harvey Mackay

■ ■ ■ ■ ■ ■ ■ ■

Mackay learned that pearl of wisdom the hard way. When asked what, if anything, he would do differently if he could start his business over, he responded that making some critical people decisions earlier topped his list.

Mackay offers his "four classic reasons" why sales managers delay firing an employee:

1. We're making money on the account.

2. Our biggest customer likes this salesperson.

3. Fire her now, and I'll have to manage this account myself for the next three months.

4. It cost us a bundle to hire and relocate this person in the first place.

Mackay isn't alone in procrastinating when it comes to employee decision-making. In fact, 78 percent of small-business owners admit to keeping an employee on staff longer then they should have, according to a 2007 survey from SurePayroll (*www.surepayroll.com*), one of America's largest full-service payroll providers and the largest online.[10] The reasons business owners keep employees too long:

■ Not being able to find an adequate replacement.

■ Giving the employee a chance to improve.

■ Fear of employee retaliation.

■ Fear of hurting the employee's feelings.

■ Fear of a lawsuit.

■ Not wanting to deal with the stress of firing.

■ Concern about office morale and empathy for the employee's personal situation.

"Firing employees is particularly difficult for business owners," says Michael Alter, SurePayroll president. "But none of the above is a good reason to avoid firing an employee if you really don't think they can improve."

SurePayroll's survey also indicates that many businesses need to address their termination practices. Of the surveyed businesses, 53 percent had no formal termination process in place. That's a big mistake, adds Alter. "If there's no rulebook on terminating employees, everything is ambiguous. That can lead to a failure to fire employees who ought to be terminated and can even lead to legal issues if terminations are viewed by employees as being unfair."

He offers the following tips on firing employees:

■ Don't let termination come as a surprise to an employee: Business owners need to let employees know what's expected of them and when they are not meeting expectations. Giving regular feedback to employees will allow you to terminate them without losing sleep if they fail to improve.

■ Offer COBRA coverage: Don't forget to offer healthcare continuation coverage as required by the federal Consolidated Omnibus Budget Reconciliation Act of 1985 (COBRA).

■ Conduct exit interviews: An exit interview with a terminated employee allows you to gather information that can be used to improve an organization's work procedures, supervisory practices, and training efforts.

Business owners surveyed by SurePayroll offer more termination tips to fellow entrepreneurs:

- When you realize there is an issue, address it immediately before it becomes an even bigger issue. If you believe that your employee is no longer an asset to your company, don't delay. Terminate immediately.
- Find good people at the start so you don't have to terminate.
- A bad attitude is contagious. Don't keep employees who have a bad attitude.
- Be objective. Don't get emotional. It's not personal; it's business.
- Keep detailed reports on every employee's performance.
- It's not fun, but it must be done. Cut your losses early.

Beyond SurePayroll.com, plenty of Websites, blogs, and organizations—maybe some you already network with—offer their take on the ups and downs of hiring and firing with tips, advice, and more. There's even a Website devoted to firings (*www.howtofireemployees.com*). A few others to check out include your local or national Better Business Bureau (or *www.BBB.org*), online HR resource Administaff's HRTools.com (*www.hrtools.com*), and the SBA (*www.sba.gov*).

Government Regulations

Many small businesses overlook the fact that, even though they're private, they operate in a strict regulatory environment, whether local, county, state, or federal. Almost everything related to employees must comply with regulations. In other words, plenty of legal nuances here and there can blindside you and your business, and sink your pocketbook, if you don't pay attention to them. That's yet another reason to hire a well-established outsource firm to do your HR or set up your own HR-designated staff member.

CableOrganizer.com still was a small home-based business operating out of Holstein's garage when he received a letter from the city telling him he needed an occupational license to do business. It was only $150, but it wasn't something Holstein had thought about when starting his company.

Certain businesses also are required to post specific posters or notices in specific places in the workplace that cover myriad topics such as safety, family and medical leaves, government contracts, nondiscrimination, and more.

It can be confusing, because not all businesses are required to post the notices. Check out the Department of Labor's Office of Small Business Program's Website (*www.dol.gov/osbp*) for a sampling of some of those rules and regulations, and how to comply with them. Don't overlook the DOL's Compliance Assistance page, either, with its direct links to specific compliance issues and solutions (*www.dol.gov/compliance*). You also can contact the DOL (1-888-9-SBREFA, or by e-mail at Contact-OSBP@dol.gov).

In case you don't think *you* can get caught up in labor-law hassles, take the following mini-quiz. You'll likely be surprised by the answers:

- **You have a great employee who works hard and is very deserving of a raise so you give it to her. Good idea or not?** No, unless you first make sure that by increasing her stipend, she, as a single mom, won't lose other government benefits. If, for example, that employee happens to receive some type of housing assistance based on income, an increase in salary can trigger a $1 for $1 reduction in those and other benefits.

U.S. Department of Labor Workplace Poster Requirements for Small Businesses and Other Employees

Poster	Who Must Post	Citations/Penalty	Other Information
Job Safety and Health Protection. Occupational Safety and Health Administration. 29 USC 657(c), 29 CFR 1903.2	Private employers engaged in a business affecting commerce. Does not apply to federal, state, or political subdivisions of states.	Any covered employer failing to post the poster may be subject to citation and penalty.	Employers in states operating OSHA-approved state plans should obtain and post the state's equivalent poster.
Equal Employment Opportunity Is the Law. Employment Standards Administration, Office of Federal Contract Compliance Programs. Executive Order 11246, as amended; Section 503 of the Rehabilitation Act of 1973, as amended; 38 U.S.C. 4212 of the Vietnam Era Veterans' Readjustment Assistance Act of 1974, as amended; 41 CFR Chapter 60-1.42; 41 CFR 60-250.4(k); 41 CFR 60-73 1.5(a)/4	Entities holding federal contracts or subcontracts or federally assisted construction contracts of $10,000 or more; financial institutions which are issuing and paying agents for U.S. savings bonds and savings notes; depositories of federal funds or entitites having government bills of lading.	Appropriate contract sacntions may be imposed for uncorrected violations.	Post copies of the poster in conspicuous places available to employees, applicants for employment, and representitives of labor organizations with which there is a collective bargaining agreement. Also, non-construction contractors or subcontractors with 50 or more employees and a contract of $50,000 or more should develop an equal opportunity policy as part of an affirmative action plan and post the policy on company boards.

Poster	Who Must Post	Citations/Penalty	Other Information
Fair Labor Standards Act (FLSA) Minimum Wage Poster. Employment Standards Administration, Wage and Hour Division.	Every private, federal, state, and local government employer employing any employee subject to the Fair Labor Standards Act, 29 USC 211, 29 CFR 516.4 posting of notices.	No citations or penalties for failure to post.	Any employer of employees to whom Sec. 7 of the Fair Labor Standards Act does not apply may alter or modify the poster legibly to show that the over-time provisions to not apply.
Employee Right for Workers With Disabilities/Special Minimum Wage Poster. Employment Standards Administration, Wage and Hour Division. 29 CFR 525.14	Every employee having workers employed under special minimum wage certificates authorized by section 14(c) of the Fair Labor Standards Act.	No citations or penalties for failure to post.	Where an employer finds it inappropriate to post such a notice, the employer may pro-vide the poster directly to all employees subject to its terms.

Poster	Who Must Post	Citations/Penalty	Other Information
Your Rights Under the Family and Medical Leave Act. Employment Standards Administration, Wage, and Hour Division. 29 CFR 825.300, .402	Public agencies (including state, local, and federal employers), public and private elementary and secondary schools, as well as private sector employers who employ 50 or more employees in 20 or more work weeks and who are engaged in commerce or in any industry or activity affecting commerce, including joint employers and successors of covered employers.	Willful refusal to post may result in a civil money penalty by the Wage and Hour Division not to exceed $100 for each separate offense.	Where an employer's workforce is not proficient in English, the employer must provide the notice in the language the employer speaks. The poster must be posted prominently where it can be readily seen by employees and applicants for employment.
Uniformed Services Employment and Reemployment Rights Act. (Notice for use by private and state employers.) Veterans' Employment and Traning Service 38 USC 4334, 20 CFR 1002	The full text of the notice must be provided by each employer to persons entitled to rights and benefits under USERRA.	No citations or penalties for failure to notify. An individual could ask USDOL to invenstigate and seek compliance, or file a private	Employers may practice the notice by posting it where employee notices are customarily placed. However, employers are free to privode the notice in other ways that will minimize costs while ensuring that the full text of the notice

Poster	Who Must Post	Citations/Penalty	Other Information
		enforcement action to require the employer to provide the notice to employees.	is provided (e.g., by distributing the notice by direct handling, mailing, or via electronic mail).
Notice to All Employees Working on Federal or Federally Financed Construction Projects (Davis-Bacon Act) Employment Standards Administration, Wage and Hour Division. 29 CFR 5.5(a)(1)	Any contractor/subcontractor engaged in contracts in excess of $2,000 for the actual construction, alteration/repair of a public building or work financed in whole or in part from federal funds, federal guarantee, or federal pledge which is subject to the labor standards provisions of any of the acts listed in 29 CFR 5.1.	No citations or penalties for failure to post.	The contractor or subcontractor is required to insert in any subcontract the poster requirements contained in 29 CFR 5.5(a)(1). The poster must be posted at the site of work, in a prominent and accesible place where it can easily be seen by workers.

Poster	Who Must Post	Citations/Penalty	Other Information
Notice to Employees Working on Government Contracts (Service Contracts Act) Employment Standards Administration, Wage and Hour Division. 29 CFR 4.6(e), .184.	Every subcontractor or subcontractor engaged in a contract with the United States or District of Columbia in excess of $2,500 the principal purpose of which is to furnish services in the U.S. through the use of service employees.	No citations or penalties for failure to post.	Contractors and any subcontractors engaged in federal service contracts exceeding $2,500 shall notify each service employee or post the minimum monetary wage and any fringe benefits required to be paid pursuant to the contract.
Notice: Employee Polygraph Protection Act Employment Standards Administration, Wage and Hour Division. 29 CFR 801.6	Any employer engaged in or affecting commerce or in the production of goods for commerce. Does not apply to federal, state, and local governments, or to circumstances covered by the national defense and security exemption.	The Secretary of Labor can bring court actions and assess civil penalties for failing to post.	The Act extends to all employees or prospective employees regardless of their citizenship status. Foreign corporations operating in the U.S. must comply or will result in penalties for failing to post. The poster must be displayed where employees can readily observe it.

Poster	Who Must Post	Citations/Penalty	Other Information
Notice Migrant and Seasonal Agricultural Worker Protection Act. Employment Standards Administration, Wage and Hour Division. 29 CFR 500.75, .76.	Agricultural employers, agricultural associations and farm labor contractors.	A civil money penalty may be assessed.	Each employer covered by the Act who provides housing to migrant agricultural workers shall post in a conspicuous place, throughout the occupancy period, information on the terms and conditions of occupancy of such housing.

Source: U.S. Department of Labor.
www.dol.gov/osbp/sbrefa/poster/matrix.htm#fmla

■ **You own a small business in Massachusetts with only a handful of employees (12 to be exact), so you don't have to offer any kind of health insurance plans to your employees. True or false?** False! Massachusetts and Hawaii are the only states that require employers to offer some kind of healthcare benefits to their employees.

■ **Even though you're a small, private business, you are subject to federal laws governing workplace safety (OSHA) and must post notices as required by law. True or false?** True. Not only are you required to post the signs, but your compliance requirements are spelled out, too. Learn more about it at the Department of Labor Website (*www.dol.gov/Compliance/Guide/Osha.Htm*).

From the Trenches

Federal, state, and even local tax and labor laws, can derail a small business if you're not up on the latest nuances or have staff or outsourcers who are. Consider a few of the laws and regulations with which we hassle regularly at the *Pacific Coast Business Times:*

■ **California labor laws:** They're complex and constantly changing, and seem arbitrary when it comes to distinguishing between salaried and hourly workers.

■ **Federal identity verification rules:** When we hire a new person, the paperwork burden is unbelievable, and includes two forms of photo ID to prove the person's identity.

■ **Payroll taxes/state unemployment insurance:** Both are extremely complicated to the point that I would not consider doing the calculations in house unless you have a specialist on staff.

■ **Local parking regulations:** With very little employee/workforce housing in downtown Santa Barbara, most of the staff drive to work. And with prohibitively expensive parking, most staff take advantage of limited free time offered at local garages. Unfortunately, that freebie block is 75 minutes, so every 75 minutes, about half my staff stops work, gets up, and disappears for 15 minutes while they move their cars.

Your Ammunition

Some essentials to remember from this chapter include:

■ You can compete for top talent if you take the HR aspect of your business seriously. Plenty of people like the freedom and personalization of a small-business employee as opposed to the corporate rat race.

■ As a small-business owner/operator, you need a good grounding in personnel management. That means management expertise and training to help you understand how to behave in ways to motivate and build trust. If you don't already have such training, get it.

■ You, what you do, how you do it, and your attitude create the corporate culture and set the tone for your small business.

■ Sources of top talent to tap include local colleges, universities, and technical schools; job banks; professional organizations; networking with other professionals and small-business owners; current employees, their friends, and their family; online organizations; and HR outsource firms.

■ You must be willing to empower your employees with the skills and responsibilities necessary to succeed.

■ Recognition and reward go a long way toward reinforcing positive returns from your employees. That doesn't always mean monetarily, either, though that does help.

CHAPTER 4

BUILDING AND MAINTAINING YOUR BRAND

Every time you, your employees, or your products touch a customer, that reflects on your brand.
—Henry Dubroff

Branding is a company's greatest asset, but a word of warning: It can be its greatest liability, too, whether you're a small business or the Big Box competition. Even though "brand" isn't a line item on the balance sheet, what customers think of your company, its products, its customer service, its employees and former employees, its community image, and even its industry standing—all part of branding—help determine the long-term success or failure of a small business.

"Branding is just a jargon term for distinctiveness," says marketing entrepreneur extraordinaire Jerry Shereshewsky, who also is CEO of Grandparents.com. We talked earlier about his unique qualifications that include development and marketing of successful products from Yahoo! to Mello Yello and Gevalia coffee. "There are many ways to think about brand, but it all comes down to how to stand out from all the other people (businesses) who are engaged in what you're engaged in."

■ ■ ■ ■ ■ ■

Branding is just a jargon term for distinctiveness.
—Jerry Shereshewsky, CEO, Grandparents.com

■ ■ ■ ■ ■ ■

Position and market your brand or image the right way, and your company will soar today and down the road. Make the wrong branding moves such as targeting the wrong audience or ignoring your image and, no matter how great or unique your product, how valuable your service, or how long your company has been established, your business will falter sooner or later. That's a guarantee.

Chances are you've already forgotten that short-lived organic restaurant down the street or that long-established, now-defunct small manufacturer across town. Do you even remember the names of these businesses? What about their unique products or services? Did you ever go to these businesses?

Most likely you answered no to these questions. What kept you away from the businesses? Or, if you tried them once or twice, why didn't you return? The answers to such questions relate to branding and the image the customer (in this case, you) has of a company and its products or services.

The Brand Impact

A strong brand with an image for integrity, dependability, quality, and fairness in the marketplace differentiates a product and, most important, grows sales for its business.

Building versus undermining your brand

The value of that brand increases every time any facet of the company touches a customer or potential customer in a positive way. Your company's image is on the line every time a customer or potential customer uses your product or services, sees your logo, hears or sees your company's name, notices its sponsorship of or participation (or lack of) in a particular event, or walks into or virtually visits your store—whether or not that customer spends any money. If prices are out of line, if customer satisfaction falters, if ads target the wrong audience, if logos don't accurately reflect your image, if a company is noticeably absent as a sponsor of an event, it all affects your brand. As the business owner, you're the keeper of that brand, so it's up to you to make the right branding moves.

The owner of the organic restaurant certainly didn't pay much attention to branding. Perhaps he assumed that his sponsorship of a butterfly exhibit at a local museum combined with his establishment's organic food concept were enough to guarantee success. It didn't matter that the restaurant's prices were a bit high and its service a bit slow. Healthy food and the location, after all, are a self-sell—only it turned out they weren't. Perhaps the former manufacturer assumed that, after all these years, he already had a strong, devoted clientele, so why bother to polish his brand or lower his prices to compete with the new guy in town? Big mistake on his part.

The restaurateur as well as the long-forgotten manufacturer discovered just how powerful brand can be. Both failed to pay enough attention to their brand and paid the ultimate price: failure. What could these companies have done differently to remain viable? Plenty, and without huge expenses, as you will see.

Hat manufacturer Imperial Headwear, as we mentioned earlier, took the cue to innovate and added value to compete, along with Kinko's, GreatHawaiiVacations.com, Tattered Cover, Craigslist.org, the *Pacific Coast Business Times*, and Frontier Airlines.

Positive differentiation

Shereshewsky uses his brother-in-law Thomas Del Spina's framing business as an example of positive differentiation of a product/service. It starts with the company's name: Thomas Del Spina Fine Frames. The Connecticut small-business man markets himself and his business as a master framer as opposed to a frame shop. He positions himself as a craftsman and is very careful about everything he does that touches the customer—from business card to invoice, and everything in between. He even borrows art masterpieces from people to display in his store. His Website *www.reproductionframes.com* describes the business:

"Thomas Del Spina Fine Frames is the purveyor—both retail and to the trade—of the most exquisite frames available."

Del Spina wants picture-framing to be a rich art experience rather than a carpentry job, says Shereshewsky. "You can go to Michael's (the arts and crafts store) and get picture-framing done, and they actually are pretty good. But they will not have the range of frames and the apparent expertise of Del Spina. He'll take a picture of your artwork and show how it looks in a particular frame on a computer screen; he will come and hang the picture, too. People pay a premium for his work, but price is almost never an issue.

"What all this does is take him out of the commodity business. There's value added to the process. Somehow Del Spina has augmented the expected and delivered generic products with enhancements on the service package that surprise and delight the customer," adds Shereshewsky.

Consider the creation and branding of Gevalia, the upscale coffee by mail that Shereshewsky helped launch. "We paid attention to every single detail," says Shereshewsky. That means from product packaging, to phone center interactions, and even the design elements in the company's invoices. All of it was designed to convey to customers that they were cared for and "cherished as a valued customer."

And those details were based on the core idea of Gevalia as a high-end product with an affordable price. The box was designed so that it looked important and could be given as a gift. How customers were treated by Gevalia's third-party phone service was key, too. "For the first four weeks after launch, we had two marketing people at the phone center all day, all night, every day, so if a phone call was for Gevalia, the operator would raise his hand and the marketing type would run over to listen and be there to help," says Shereshewsky. "We didn't want to give any customer a bad Gevalia experience."

"It's got to look good or else they'll know you're a fake," adds Del Spina.

From the Trenches

I found out firsthand the power of a name as a brand soon after I started the *Pacific Coast Business Times*. Early on I was slightly embarrassed at the prospect of creating my own company, especially one with a name like *Pacific Coast Business Times*, which was a mouthful. I wasn't even sure how to pronounce it with the right cadence or which word to emphasize. Perhaps my inability to articulate the name reflected my doubts about whether it would ever succeed.

But a chance meeting with Dave Spainhour, then chairman of Pacific Capital Bancorp., parent of Santa Barbara Bank & Trust, the largest bank in our region, proved me wrong. It was a few months after we had launched the newspaper, and of course we were losing buckets of money.

I ran into Spainhour, a strong proponent of our publication, in the parking lot at a nearby bank branch. He was there with another community bigwig and went out of his way to introduce me as the owner of The *Pacific Coast Business Times*. He said the words definitively; he didn't try to embellish or add anything, but said the mouthful as if the company had been around for years.

Wow, I thought. *That's the way I should say it.* From then on, I copied Spainhour's carefully cadenced pronunciation of my company's name. It inspired confidence in me and in the venture, and I count that as the day when our brand really took on a life of its own. I learned much later that the bank actually had done a study that identified the lack of a business publication as one of the region's economic weaknesses.

Costs and returns

Most small companies can't afford to pay much for help with branding their company, nor should they. Don't, however, fall into the small-business trap and think branding doesn't matter. More than half (55 percent) of small-business owners/managers said that their business didn't need much marketing because their products and services pretty much sell themselves; 42 percent disagreed, according to a survey from the NFIB Research Foundation.[1] In that same study, 48 percent of small businesses indicated they have a separate annual marketing budget within the firm's overall budget, while 43 percent did not.

As a small-business owner, you had better not sit back and wait for your customers to beat down your door. Customers always have other options.

Newtonian marketing

Small businesses should think about and approach marketing with Sir Isaac Newton's laws of motion in mind, says Shereshewsky:

- An object in motion tends to stay in motion unless an external force is applied. By the same token, an object at rest remains at rest unless acted on by an external force. "Very large companies going nowhere keep going nowhere, while a tiny company with a lot of motion or forward momentum can push the Big Box out of business," adds Shereshewsky. "That means a big company that's stagnant will stay that way, while a small company that's energized and moving forward will continue to do so unless someone screws it up!"

- For every action there is an equal and opposite reaction, wrote Newton. "Don't expect your actions to go unanswered," says Shereshewsky. "Starbucks didn't, neither did IBM or Xerox. (All three companies reacted late to the small upstarts, but they reacted nonetheless.) From a business survival standpoint, no matter the size of a business, nothing is going to change unless you do something pretty dramatic. And once you've got things going well, you need to offset competing forces that will try to negate the change," adds Shereshewsky.

For example, consider the dry-cleaning company that gives its customers bags imprinted with its name. In Internet jargon, that's called "stickiness," because it's a way to draw the customer back to that business. The dry cleaner picks up its clients' dirty clothes every Tuesday and Thursday, and returns them clean the following week. With its *stickiness* and value-added service in the form of convenient pickup and delivery, the business is moving forward. Then the competition does something that upsets or stalls things. In this case, the competition decides to pick up dirty clothes at the end of the workweek, Friday evening, and return them cleaned and pressed by Sunday evening before the new workweek begins. "In this case a service enhancement has aced out a product advantage," adds Shereshewsky.

Navigating the Customer Divide

As small-business owners, many of our ideas about branding come from experiences with marketing to consumers. That means advertising at traditional times in traditional venues such as local newspapers and radio, and then tailoring information and events to the typical bricks-and-mortar consumer shopping experiences.

Seven in 10 business owners believed their marketing investments were effective in promoting growth, but fewer than half reported a direct uptick in sales from their marketing efforts, according to the Fall 2007 American Express OPEN Small Business Monitor, a semi-annual survey of business owners.[2]

That's a good starting point, but it's only part of the story. Another big part is the business-to-business experience, which can be very different and very lucrative. In fact, worldwide, business-to-business sales are the main driver for millions of small businesses ranging from accounting and law firms to copy services, niche manufacturers, and IT services. Some businesses, such as CableOrganizer.com even end up straddling the business-to-business and business-to-company fence servicing both markets.

How you find and capitalize on the market for your goods or services depends on you, your business, your business's structure, and plenty more.

Identify your market

No matter what your business or budget, branding and marketing both start with one essential question: What market does my company serve? In other words, who are your *primary* customers, consumers, or businesses? Who uses or will use your products or services, and how will they use them? The questions sound clear enough, although the answers may not be. The answers, however, are a bottom-line secret to building a successful branding strategy.

■ ■ ■ ■ ■ ■

Know your market first.

■ ■ ■ ■ ■ ■

Remember in Chapter 2 when CableOrganizer.com's Holstein opened a storefront in a location that didn't attract his target market, which he belatedly learned was other businesses? He made his initial move before he had truly identified his target customer base, and integrated that information into his business strategy.

If you identify who your customers are and then make savvy marketing moves, it's possible to dominate and prosper in a small but significant piece of the market—whatever your market—as long as you have a solid product or service. The classic examples are specialty retailers such as the nail salon, kids' clothing store, and metropolitan-area restaurant, each of which recognizes its specific market, caters to it, markets to it, and prospers as a result.

Consider small-business owner Dan Diaz. His Familia Diaz restaurant in Santa Paula, California, has been operating since 1936. When Diaz took over the family operation, the restaurant's customer base was aging and prospects for new customers appeared threatened by all the trendy new Mexican restaurants in the area. Instead of trying to target those same consumers and compete with literally dozens of other restaurants in his part of Southern California, Diaz looked to the region's huge untapped business-to-business market. Of course, he still welcomed the regular consumer trade, but Diaz began to focus his branding efforts toward the business consumer.

To differentiate himself and the name recognition of his brand, Diaz became a driving force on the board of directors of the local chamber of commerce. He and his restaurant hosted business events. Recognizing the importance of the Latino culture to his customers, Diaz also became a big player in the development of a citrus festival in Southern California that brought in big Latino stars. All this meant more business for his restaurant and a solid future for the growing Familia Diaz.

Who are your customers?

As we've discussed, your branding efforts must reach your potential customers. Who is and who is NOT that customer? That's essential to know so you can tailor and target your message.

Diaz identified businesses as a prime audience. Sometimes, however, despite research, a business may not recognize who its primary potential customers truly are. Frontier Airlines thought its success lay in one market when it was reborn in Denver in 1994. The company at first branded itself as a regional carrier that would service underserved rural and other areas of the West. The airline struggled to compete until it recognized that its real customer base—hence revenue stream—was a much broader business and consumer audience, and that success lay in competing as a low-cost carrier in a broader market. The company re-branded itself, and the rest is a tale of success. That success, though, has met plenty of bumps in the road. Tough economic times forced Frontier into Chapter 11 bankruptcy reorganization in April 2008.

Identify how or why customers use your product or service

You must know who your customer is, but that alone is not enough. It's also essential that any company find out why and how its target audience uses its product, says Wolfe, the veteran Coca-Cola executive who took over as CEO of a fledgling nutritional supplement company in 1995. "So do your research," he adds. "We did and it paid off handsomely."

When Wolfe took over what became Balance Bar, sales were less than $1 million and the company had considered folding. Only five years later, Wolfe, with his branding genius, had turned the company into a major market player that giant Kraft Inc. paid $268 million to acquire. Not a bad payoff for a few years' work!

To create such a mega-success, Balance Bar went beyond simply identifying the market and customers its product served. It examined how its product was being used by those customers. It turned out that the then-struggling company was marketing/branding its product to the wrong audience!

As wild as that sounds, such a faux pas isn't all that uncommon. Companies often make assumptions about how their products are used, says Wolfe. Reality then intervenes and shows those assumptions to be invalid.

Wolfe's bar originally was developed by Bio Foods Inc. as a supplement for people such as diabetics with special dietary needs as well as those concerned with weight loss. But Wolfe knew that his bar was superior in content and taste to the competition. He wondered whether the bar could have much broader mass consumer appeal if it were marketed as a snack bar.

"When I took over, the company wasn't doing well, and so I was questioning why not? Is it that we're not appealing to the right target market? Do we know for certain that the people who are buying the bar are in fact using it as a weight loss or diabetic bar, or are they buying it for a different reason entirely? We didn't really have any research on the product that identified who our primary user was," says Wolfe.

Wolfe recognized that the company needed solid market research from its existing customers if it hoped to improve its balance sheet. That meant knowing who was buying the product, how they were using it, who in a particular household was using it, as well as demographic information to enhance marketing efforts. Because the company was struggling, there wasn't a big budget for such research, and the Internet wasn't yet the great tool it is today.

As Wolfe proved, though, market research for a small business needn't cost tons of money or involve expensive outsourcers. Because the company marketed directly to consumers, it had a mailing list of existing customers. Because Wolfe had plenty of prior experience in marketing and consumer research through his work at Coca-Cola, Welch's, and other companies, he was able to design a questionnaire to send to those customers. To encourage customers to return the questionnaire, the company offered to send a free box of bars in exchange. Brilliant! Seventy-five percent of the customers who received the questionnaire responded.

The results: People primarily liked the bar as a snack and meal replacement. That meant changing how the bar was sold, what the product should taste like, and what the packaging should look like, too.

The company had only a small marketing budget—typically 10 percent of its revenues, says Wolfe—but it put that budget to work the right way. Instead of direct marketing to special-needs consumers, the company began marketing to retailers and distributors to attract its new target. Instead of spending big bucks on flashy TV advertising or handing out bars on street corners and wasting cash on consumers who didn't fit its potential niche, Balance Bar also identified venues and events that drew this target market and began to sponsor those events and offer free product samples. For taste-tests of various products, the company would set up a card table in front of a local natural food store and offer the products for feedback. Natural food retailers such as Wild Oats, Whole Foods, and Trader Joe's were a natural fit for their marketing efforts.

"These were easy places to get target consumers to try our product," says Wolfe.

"In the beginning, some people resisted even trying the product because our competitor Power Bar did great marketing but didn't taste very good. But once people tasted our product, they wanted more. That led almost overnight to soaring sales. We paid attention to building a strong brand from the get-go," adds Wolfe. "We made sure that all the different people we touched—from brokers and suppliers to consumers—were happy with us and our product."

The rest is branding history.

■ ■ ■ ■ ■ ■ ■ ■

How to Identify Your Market

Some questions to ask and answer honestly to help you recognize the real market for your product or services include:

- *What problem/issue does your product/service solve? For whom/what?*
- *Who can benefit the most from your product/service?*
- *Is the beneficiary a business or consumer?*
- *Does the product/service serve other businesses or consumers?*
- *Is its existing use/market the highest and best use of the product/service?*
- *Are other potential markets possibly more lucrative?*
- *How might your product/service serve that market?*
- *If yours is an existing product/service, who are your primary customers today?*
- *Who might be your primary customers in the future?*

■ ■ ■ ■ ■ ■ ■ ■ ■

Beyond the obvious

Similar to Wolfe's company, small businesses—new and established—often find themselves flailing about, barely making it and unsure of their future because they haven't really differentiated whether their real and consistent customers are other businesses or individual consumers. Whatever your business, don't make assumptions. It's essential to determine who your true customers are, so you can successfully tailor your message, your brand, and your marketing to that segment.

When George Wolverton took over as advertising sales director of my fledgling business journal, the advertising department was thrashing about in the woods, looking for customers, as he puts it. The staff basically was wasting its time knocking on doors of every possible retailer and small local business, figuring the more ground they covered, the more ads they would sell. Wolverton recognized, though, that to find advertisers required careful and thorough research. Instead of the corner store, those advertisers likely would come from the ranks of traditional business-journal advertisers—those companies with a vested interest and looking for big returns on their advertising dollar. That meant commercial banks, large law firms, accounting firms, commercial real estate brokerages, insurance agencies, and other companies engaged in a business-to-business marketplace. Why? Because the *Pacific Coast Business Times'* real and consistent customers were other businesses. We are primarily a business-to-business publication.

Take the time to think about who your customer's truly are; you might be surprised.

Outside consultants can help

Today you have plenty of options to help accurately determine your market, your customers, and your strategies. Simply paying attention to who walks by your store, picks up your product, or is interested in promoting your product or service can be an indication, or at least a starting point. If I had paid a bit closer attention, it might have saved me a few headaches—and some cash—with the *Pacific Coast Business Times*.

But don't rule out the cost of really and truly identifying your customer. If it means paying an additional fee for a formal survey, pay it. As the efforts of Wolfe and others reflect, you shouldn't assume such a survey will cost you big bucks. You can have online surveys done by groups such as Zoomerang (*www.zoomerang.com*); you can create your own survey with software tools from SurveyMonkey.com (*www.surveymonkey.com*); or you might hire any of a number of consultant organizations—local, regional, national, or international—that specialize in identifying markets and customer bases.

Don't, however, make the big (and costly) mistake of running out in a panic to identify your customers. Knee-jerk reactions don't pay. I learned that the hard way. Instead, be methodical and careful about identifying your markets and be selective in who you get to help you. When we launched the *Pacific Coast Business Times*, I was desperate to expand our circulation and figured I absolutely had to have an expensive consulting service identify those customers right this minute. In a panic I paid way too much for outside expertise and got very little in return.

That doesn't mean you shouldn't hire someone to help identify your customers. On the contrary, such an expenditure can make good sense, depending on your business. But do your homework first, and then thoroughly check out any potential consulting services. Make sure their clients are highly satisfied with their work before you shell out the cash.

What you can do to help

Before you pay someone to identify your customers, ask yourself who those customers are and how they use your product or services. Sit down with a pad of paper and pencil or at the keyboard, and be honest in your answers. Record your responses so they can help you better recognize your core customers and, in turn, formulate an effective marketing plan.

Some things to consider, according to SCORE's Lehman, are:

- Is anyone who walks past your store or down the street a potential customer?
- Do customers buy your product or services for work or leisure purposes?
- Are your primary customers male, female, or both?
- Does your primary customer have total control over how he or she spends his or her money?
- What differentiates you from your competitors?
- Do your customers buy your product once or will they be repeat customers?

All these considerations make a difference in how you brand your product. If, for example, your business relies on repeat customers, you will need to devote more effort and resources toward customer relations management (CRM).

Don't get off track if, when you really consider it, your customers seem to be split between regular consumers and other businesses. Consider re-examining your core customer base. Could it be that you're really a business-to-business company? An auto body shop, for example, may get business from walk-in consumers, but ultimately its core customers are insurance companies, which are other businesses.

21st-Century Marketing

In the branding and marketing battle today, the teams are the same—it's still you versus the competition in the fight for the customer. The battlefield is bigger, but basically the same—it's now global, wired, and more. Only the tactics truly have changed.

Charitable marketing

Domino's franchisee Hishmeh identified his customers up front and decided to target market, but with a twist. Similar to Diaz, he opted to generate business by becoming a driving community force, taking steps to link his brand with the community because, after all, his customers are the community. He refers to his community involvement, putting his company's dollars into the local community, as *charitable marketing.* "I serve on nine different nonprofit boards, and through those boards I meet a lot of people. The impression I like to leave is that Domino's is a community partner. Part of the money you spend with us will go back to the community," says Hishmeh.

That's how Hishmeh has chosen to brand and market his company. "In most businesses it's a very competitive environment," he says. "You have to separate yourself. Everyone gives good service, good product, and good prices. They have to because, if they don't, it's only a matter of time until they go out of business. So how do you differentiate yourself? We're a community partner."

The upside and the downside of that partnership, says Hishmeh, is that it works. The benefit to the community is the upside. Unlike traditional types of marketing such as print or broadcast media, however, community involvement takes time to net results. That's the downside. Hishmeh is in his second year of volunteerism and just starting to see its tangible results in his business. "You don't go out and get involved in the community during the day and see your stores ring up sales that night," he says.

Marketing through community involvement isn't right for every small business, either. It's time-consuming, and not all owners/operators can spare the time away from the day-to-day operations of their business. "I have a unique structure in my company because I have a lot of family running the company. I don't have to pay much attention to that, so I have the time to dedicate to community involvement," Hishmeh says. "This marketing/branding model could work for any company with a good operational system in place so you (the owner) have the time to get out and get involved in the community."

We're in partnership with the community, too, at the *Pacific Coast Business Times*. It's an important role for us because our market is the community we live in and depend on for information, advertising, and interest. Community involvement is vital to us.

Similar to Diaz, Wolfe, Hishmeh, and others, no matter your budget, you can brand for your company's success with the right approach. Your company's brand and who you and your company are differentiate you.

Combating impersonalization

In the early part of the 20th century, all marketing was personal, says Shereshewsky. You walked into a store, and the guy behind the counter knew you and likely ran a tab for you. If you needed clothes, you went to your personal tailor; if you wanted to send flowers, you went to the florist who called you by name; and so on. In the early part of the 21st century, however, much of that personal touch has gone the way of the dinosaur. Mass marketing generally isn't conducive to that level of personalization.

But that's where, yet again, small is big! That's where and how small businesses can differentiate themselves—by bringing back that level of personalization. "That's the difference between your restaurant and someone else's restaurant," says Shereshewsky. "It isn't just the food. You have to have good food, or you'll be out of business in a week. The difference is how the restaurant takes care of *me*. Does the maître d' remember me? Do I get progressively better tables? If I come into the restaurant on a jammed Friday night, do I get seated because he remembers that I've been there 14 times?"

"It's the addition of value, these augmentations to the product that surprise and delight the consumer, that mean everything—especially in a business-to-business environment," he adds.

Your personal brand

You, the business owner, can be the brand, too. Shereshewsky, with his track record for success and sales, is a great example. "I'm very much in a business where I make sales to people because they know me, like me, and trust me," he says of his new position as CEO of startup Grandparents.com.

"I cannot compete in the marketplace right now with numbers. I don't have a big enough audience. But I have signed deals with Johnson & Johnson, Hasbro, and Pepsi Cola.... They didn't have to buy (advertising at) Grandparents.com," he says. "In fact, it's risky for them to spend 10 cents with us right now. We are not a big proven entity with millions of visitors. We're 150,000 visitors a month and growing, yet I got Pepsi to sign a piece of paper because I added value to the sale: the relationship I have with the guy who made the decision. I am a brand. I am as much a brand as anything and everything else you can imagine."

On a smaller scale, I was a brand, too, when I decided to pursue the entrepreneurial route and start the *Pacific Coast Business Times*. I was able to pick up financial backers because of my brand as a successful, reliable, conscientious business editor with a sense of business and great ideas. Of course, my business plan didn't hurt, either (we'll get into that later). Nonetheless, my brand figured into the picture, too.

Hishmeh is his own brand, as is Craigslist's Newmark, TV chef/restaurateur Emeril Lagasse, and the list goes on.

Cherish the repeat customer

When the *Pacific Coast Business Times* launched, we already had a small circulation from the predecessor paper we purchased. The numbers certainly weren't enough to sustain our vision of a local business journal, but they represented a starting point, and we knew it. We kept our few existing subscribers well informed of our plans, and we did our best to satisfy them. Similar to any small business, we couldn't then or now afford to lose customers.

"If you own or buy an older company that has great brand recognition but a little tarnish on its finish, it's a safe bet there's a cadre of loyal customers eager to re-establish their connection," adds entrepreneur/author Mackay.

Hishmeh had a basic formula to build sales at his 15 Domino's franchise outlets, which, incidentally, are among the pizza chain's top 10 percent in volume today.

"I tell my managers we have to do what it takes to not lose any customers—good food, quality food, treat them like you care, and our national marketing should take care of bringing in new customers, along with my local marketing."

Another approach to marketing brings back customers for more, but not necessarily by advertising in the newspaper. Instead, it involves offering product discounts and a punch card that provides a free product after so many visits or so many dollars spent. It's a favorite tool used by neighborhood coffee bistros, whether franchise outlets or single-store locations. But it's by no means strictly the purview of latte purveyors. Razzle Toys, a small toy store in suburban Denver, successfully buys into the punch card marketing approach and has a loyal string of customers, too. At $20 a punch, filling the card requires 10 punches, or $200 spent at the store. In return, customers then receive $15 off their next purchase.

On the flip side of marketing to frequent customers is the diamond merchant who expends his branding efforts on flashy advertising to attract customers for what generally is a one-time diamond purchase.

GreatHawaiiVacations.com, which in today's tough economic times still thrives with the help of its repeat customers, emphasizes valued-added customer service to differentiate itself from the competition and keep customers coming back. One of its clients recounted to me disappointing service at a well-known Hawaii destination resort. When Goldberg learned of the client's disappointment, she immediately—without being asked—went to the resort staff and demanded and got compensation for the client in the form of a discount for future stays. That's customer service. That's differentiation. That's a dependable brand taken very seriously.

Don't hesitate to periodically do market research relating to your repeat customers, either. As the reach of your product or service grows or shrinks and your demographics change, so too can how and why your company's product or service is used.

"My product is my primary advertising," says master framer Del Spina. But his passion for his business and his customer relationship management keep his customers coming back, and they do so in droves to pay $80 to $100 a foot for handmade custom period picture frames. That's compared with only $10 to $50 a linear foot for frames from "the other guys."

"There are days when my cell phone battery can't last a day," he says. But Del Spina is not on the phone constantly selling product to his customers, either. He's helping them, too. "My customers say to me, 'I can't believe how enthusiastic you are about your product.' They don't just buy a frame. They call me up and ask for my help. I draw pictures. I walk them through it, and I never charge for all the service that I supply because this is the reason they buy so many frames from me—the support I lend my customers."

■ ■ ■ ■ ■ ■ ■ ■ ■

We made sure that all the different people we touched—from brokers and suppliers to consumers—were happy with us and our product.
—Jim Wolfe, former CEO, Balance Bar

■ ■ ■ ■ ■ ■ ■ ■ ■

Collaborative marketing

Open your eyes and mind to the possibility of working to market your business with other small businesses in your area—whether they compete with you for the same consumer dollars or not. That could mean working with business or industry groups and associations or even banding together with your fellow small-business competitors.

■ ■ ■ ■ ■ ■ ■ ■

Love your competitors. They are the only ones who make you as good as you can be.
—Harvey Mackay

■ ■ ■ ■ ■ ■ ■ ■

That kind of a relationship may not work for every situation, but consider how collaborative marketing helped fuel success for Denver-based entrepreneur Hickenlooper's brewpubs. "Everyone told us the restaurant business was so cutthroat," says Hickenlooper. Yet when he and his partners opened their brewpub in a then-run-down area of lower downtown Denver, they recognized that they first needed to get the word out that the area itself could be a dinner destination. "We started putting ads up in our hallway and our restrooms that advertised our competitors," says Hickenlooper. "My staff got sort of upset and asked, 'Why are you advertising your opponents?' I said, 'Well you know in the end, our real competition is the TV set, and our job is to get people off the couch and out the door to enjoy life with their friends and their family. So if we do our job but sometimes they go down to McCormick's Fish House (down the street) and sometimes they go down to the Wazee Supper Club (also down the street), if we do our job, we'll get our share.' If all of these restaurants are working together, it will be a rising tide."

Hickenlooper's approach worked, and his restaurants thrived. Collaborative marketing could pay dividends for your business, too.

Tricky business of events management

Wolfe and his Balance Bar team were at the forefront of events management and became experts in this booming field. They knew how to select the event that targeted their exact demographic and how to execute the sponsorship, taste-testing, and more with marketing and branding precision. Market research showed that Balance Bar's customers were typically college-educated, upper-middle class, and upper income, and people who were nutritionally aware, says Wolfe. That meant Balance Bar was a frequent sponsor of health fairs, bicycle races, jazz festivals, tennis events, and even a rock-and-roll marathon. Tractor pulls, on the other hand, weren't a big draw for Balance Bar's demographics, and consequently the company wasn't a sponsor.

Wolfe suggests that companies think about the following when deciding whether to sponsor or participate in a particular event:

- Will there be enough people at that particular event who are within your target audience?
- Is there an opportunity that allows potential customers to try your product?
- Will you have the opportunity to discuss your goods/ services with a captive audience as potential customers?
- Will you have the opportunity to capture contact information for potential customers?

Pay particular attention to the target audience of an event and how it may or may not relate to your target demographic. At the *Pacific Coast Business Times*, for example, we sponsor the Spirit of Small Business Awards annually, and have done so since 2003. They're both an innovation that keeps our community interested in us and a marketing tool that enhances our brand.

It sounds like a perfectly orchestrated brand bonanza. Instead, the awards are the result of a series of happy accidents. In 2003, we were looking for an exciting new editorial product to jazz up our summer, and the Los Angeles District office of the U.S. SBA needed a partner to launch an outreach effort in Santa Barbara and Ventura counties in California. So we teamed to develop a special newspaper report that combines profiles of exemplary companies, a how-to guide for small-business owners, and a list of business resources from all the communities in our region. Meanwhile, the politicians and movers and shakers in our area were hungry for a new event that would take place in August to jump-start the fall political season. The result was the Spirit Awards, held every year in August. Our kickoff lunch back then received an extra boost, too, when Hector Baretto, then–SBA chief, came out from Washington, D.C., to personally provide the keynote address. Today the awards—and the positive branding that accompanies them—honor eight small businesses in the area, and 500 or more people show up to attend the awards luncheon.

The "e" factor

Getting your message out to your customers has gotten a whole lot easier, and in many ways cheaper, too, with the advent of new technologies that enhance how we communicate. As with any aspect of differentiating your small business so that it stands out, there's a right and a wrong way to use the technologies to promote your product. Think quality instead of quantity, urges Rogers.

Forget the blast faxes, e-mails, and text messages. Instead, look for innovative ways to draw in your customers. Rogers recounts a tale of one new restaurant in New York City that opened with a paltry $35,000 ad budget. Instead of spending that on a small, traditional ad that likely would have been buried in a newspaper, the restaurant posted simple fliers around the neighborhood advertising the grand opening, and offering a free burrito. That was it. Customers came in droves, enjoyed the free product, talked, texted, or e-mailed their friends about it, and the restaurant became a hit. "As customers are freer to talk to each other in a more empowered way with the Internet and more, we need to see small businesses take advantage of that," adds Rogers.

Tough Economic Times

Don't use today's tough economics as an excuse to slash your marketing or event sponsorship, either. Figure a way financially (more on that in Chapter 6 to get it done, and done right).

When times get tough, a lot of companies trim costs and cut down on marketing products, says Hishmeh. "I believe when things are tough, this is a time to maintain or even increase your marketing spending because the best way to improve profits is to improve sales. Cutting costs improves profits short term. On the other hand increasing sales improves profit long-term."

But beware, he cautions. Never start trimming marketing dollars or your overhead without expecting a negative outcome unless it's only extra fat you're cutting out of your business. That's okay, he says.

Your Ammunition

Some essentials to remember from this chapter include:
- Branding is simply jargon for how you differentiate yourself and your company from the competition.
- That differentiation is key. Without it, you cannot succeed long-term. You must stand out and exceed

your competitors, whether with your product, service, approach, personalization, something else entirely, or better yet, all of the above.

■ Keep in mind that every time anything related to you or your business—including your employees—touches a customer, it reflects on your brand.

■ Your brand starts with knowing what your market is and who are your customers are. Find that out with the right kind of research. With that information you're then able to tailor your marketing and branding to that audience in the way that best serves them.

■ Beware, however: Potential customers will recognize any branding or marketing that doesn't reflect your business.

CHAPTER
5

YOUR CUSTOMERS AND EFFECTIVE SALES

There's a sign on my office conference table that reads: Our meeting will not be interrupted...unless a customer calls.
—Harvey Mackay

Sales are the oxygen supply for your business. Customers generate those sales. Lose those customers, and you cut off the oxygen, lose the sales, and choke your business. It's that simple—period.

How often have you as a consumer ended up at a Big Box to buy a product because of better prices or a better return policy than the small business down the street offers? Or, conversely, how often do you walk out of a Big Box because of an employee's or, worse yet, a manager's impersonal attitude? How about that service provider who didn't bother to return your calls? Did you call back time and again? Probably not. In each of these scenarios, you likely went elsewhere with your business. Whether your company offers goods or services, your customers are likely to go elsewhere, too, if you don't meet or exceed their expectations. Don't ever forget that customers have choices, and plenty of them.

Grandparents.com's Shereshewsky recounts a riddle he frequently posed to employees during his tenure at Yahoo! as ambassador plenipotentiary to Madison Avenue. "I would ask the salespeople, 'What does the word *Yahoo* mean?' They would come up with some ridiculous answer, and my response would be, '*Yahoo* to the customer reminds them that You Always Have Other Options.' There is nobody who has an automatic guaranteed lock on the business," says Shereshewsky. "In the B-to-B business, you can always buy around anybody. If you are a fancy retailer and one of your clothing lines treats you badly, you can do very well never carrying another piece of that merchandise in your store. You can always buy around them. What you can't do is lose the customer, because it's the customer who's the source of your business."

"If you are a consultant, what are you selling? You're selling service; you're selling, 'Yes, I answer the phone at 10 at night' and 'Yes, I understand the elephant ate the report I sent you, I'll send another one over right away.' You do whatever has to be done because it is the relationship between you and the customer that is so important. In small business and in small business-to-business, that importance is only attenuated," he adds.

Let's take a closer look.

Sales in Context

Sales typically happen in a strategic context. They may be the result of relationships established between purchaser and provider, or they may be the result of intelligence gathered about a product or service and its provider. Whatever the case, the provider truly understands and meets the customer's need. Simply put, sales come from knowing your customer, knowing your product, and consistently providing the right kind of product and personalized service.

For many small businesses, the repeat customer can make a vital difference. According to a 2007 poll from the NFIB:[1]

- 12 percent of small-business owners indicate virtually all customers are repeat customers.
- 35 percent say most customers are repeat customers.
- 45 percent say their customer base is a mix of repeat and non-repeat customers.
- 3 of 4 small employers say repeat customers are prized because they are easier to attract than new ones.
- 7 of 10 employers say it's cheaper to retain repeat customers than obtain new ones.

The customer connection

People—not specs on a product or deal—are the key to determining who gets the sale, says entrepreneur and author Mackay, who transformed a tiny envelope company into a giant, in large part by making solid customer relationships a top priority.

"Salespeople and customers or potential customers can't talk about business 100 percent of the time," Mackay adds. "Most interchanges between salespeople and customers are 30 to 35-percent business and 65 to 70 percent social. People buy from other people because of likeability, chemistry, and people skills." He adds, "Of course, you also must perform—actually, outperform—and build the relationship, too. If you do that, you not only will get the order, but you'll get all the reorders. That means you'd better pay attention to what the other person is in the market for, do it sincerely, and use the information to build a long-term relationship. That's what you're really after, not a one-shot victory."

To that end, MackayMitchell uses the Mackay 66 questionnaire to gather data about customers and their personal and business preferences and interests.

■■■■■■■■■

The Mackay 66 Customer Profile

It's critical to have information about your customer. Armed with the right knowledge, you can outsell, outmanage, outmotivate, and outnegotiate your competition. Knowing your customer means knowing what your customer really wants. Maybe it's your product, but maybe there is something else, too: recognition, respect, reliability, service, friendship, help—things all of us care more about as human beings than we care about envelopes. Once you attach your personality to the proposition, people start reacting to the personality and stop reacting to the proposition.

Use this questionnaire to develop a profile of each customer. Some of your resources for the information might include receptionists, suppliers, newspapers, assistants, trade publications, and the customers themselves. Look, listen, and learn all you can about the customer, both personally and professionally. You'll find topics for opening conversations, which can open doors for you and your company.

Date

Customer

1. *Name:*

   Nickname:

2. *Company name:*

3. *Address:*

   Home address:

4. *Telephone:*

   Business:

   Home:

5. *Birthdate:*

   Place:

   Hometown:

6. *Height (approx.):*
   Weight (approx.):

Education

7. *High school:*
   Year graduated:
   College:
   Year graduated:
8. *College honors:*
   Degrees:
9. *College fraternity/sorority:*
   Sports:
10. *College extracurricular activities:*
11. *If customer didn't attend college, is he/she sensitive about it?*
12. *Military service:*
    Discharge rank:
    Attitude toward being in the service:

Family

13. *Spouse's name and occupation:*
14. *Spouse's education:*
15. *Spouse's interests:*
16. *Anniversary:*
17. *Children if any (names/ages):*
18. *Children's education:*
19. *Children's interest (hobbies, problems, etc.):*

Business Background

20. *Previous employment (most recent first):*
    Company:

Location:
Title:
Dates:
Company:
Location:
Title:
Dates:

21. *Previous positions at present company:*
    Title:
    Dates:
22. *"Status" symbols in office:*
23. *Professional/trade:*
24. *Offices held or honors:*
25. *What business relationship does he/she have with others in our company?*
26. *Who are they?*
27. *Is it a good relationship? Why?*
28. *Who else in our company knows the customer?*
29. *Type of connection:*
    Name of relationship:
30. *What do you feel is his/her long-range business objective?*
31. *What do you feel is his/her immediate business objective?*
32. *What do you think is of greatest concern to the customer at this time—the welfare of the company or his/her own personal welfare?*
33. *Does the customer think of the present or the future?*

Special interests

34. Clubs, fraternal associations or service clubs (Masons, Kiwanis, etc.)

35. Politically active?

    Party

    Important to customer?

36. Active in community? How?

37. Religion

    Active?

38. Highly confidential/sensitive items not to be discussed with customer (i.e., divorce, AA member, etc.)

39. On what subjects (outside of business) does the customer have strong feelings?

Lifestyle

40. Medical history (current condition of health):

41. Does customer drink? If yes, what and how much?

42. If no, is customer offended by others drinking?

43. Does customer smoke? If no, object to others?

44. Favorite places for lunch:

    Dinner:

45. Favorite items on menu:

46. Does customer object to having anyone buy his/her meal?

47. Hobbies and recreational interests:

48. Vacation habits:

49. Spectator sports interest (sports and teams):

50. What kind of car(s):

51. Conversational interests:

52. Whom does the customer seem anxious to impress?

53. *How does he/she want to be seen by those people?*
54. *What adjectives would you use to describe the customer?*
55. *What is he/she most proud of having achieved?*
56. *What do you feel is the customer's long-range personal objective?*
57. *What do you feel is the customer's immediate personal goal?*

The Customer and You

58. *What moral or ethical considerations are involved when you work with this customer?*
59. *Does the customer feel any obligation to you, your company or your competition? If so, what?*
60. *Does the proposal you plan to make to him/her require the customer to change a habit or take an action that is contrary to custom?*
61. *Is he/she primarily concerned about the opinion of others?:*
62. *Is he/she very self-centered?*
    Highly ethical?
63. *What are the key problems as the customer sees them?*
64. *What are the priorities of the customer's management?*
65. *Can you help with these problems?*
66. *Does your competitor have better answers to the above questions than you have?*

Source: Harvey Mackay, www.harveymackay.com; MackayMitchell Envelope Company.[2]

■ ■ ■ ■ ■ ■ ■ ■ ■

Of course, not every small business owner takes the time to learn about his or her customers and his or her lives the way Harvey Mackay does. Not all small business owners are as successful as Mackay, either. Think of the market research efforts of Balance Bar's Wolfe and his subsequent product success, too.

■ ■ ■ ■ ■ ■ ■

People don't care how much you know about them once they realize how much you care about them.

—Harvey Mackay, writer, author, entrepreneur

■ ■ ■ ■ ■ ■ ■ ■ ■

Whatever the time and effort invested, though, successful small-business owners must make the effort to know their customers and establish relationships with them. It's an extension of marketing your brand that we talked about in the last chapter.

In our businesses, it's called the schmooze factor. Get to know the news source, and you have a better chance of getting the story; sponsor the right event, and the community will get to know you better and vice versa; become friendly with advertisers so you understand their goals, and you will be better able to serve their needs; and so on.

Domino's franchise success story Hishmeh takes very seriously the importance of getting to know, connecting with, and listening to his customers. "Listen to what they are telling you, because that's an indicator of what you are doing right and not. Last week we raised our prices 10 percent because of cost increases. This week I met with managers to find out the customer feedback and decided whether I made a bad decision and need to retract it."

■■■■■■■■

Measuring and tracking customer satisfaction and service quality can be as easy as making sure you're in touch with the customer.
—James D. (Jamey) Power IV, senior vice president and strategic advisor, J.D. Power and Associates

■■■■■■■■

Quality and customer service starts from the top, says James D. (Jamey) Power IV, senior vice president and strategic advisor for J.D. Power and Associates, *the* leader in assessing quality in products and service. "It's got to start with leadership, and whether the leadership of the organization has the passion for focusing on quality and customer service," says Power. "Without that, it doesn't hold together." Power should know, too. His firm, founded by his father, J.D. Power, sets the standard for quality when it comes to products and services, especially in the auto industry.

Measuring whether your product or service stands up doesn't necessarily take scientific surveys either, says Power. It's as simple as staying in touch with your customers perhaps with an e-mail or other sort of reminder to solicit feedback. When you get that feedback, says Power, "the next challenge then is to sort through it and do something with it!"

In the publishing business, for example, says Power, if customers don't renew, find out why not. "Your escaped customer is an overlooked source of information."

It begins and ends with service

The three crucial elements to keeping your customer satisfied are service, service, and service, says Mackay. "If you can't compete on price, then it's logical to compete with more services or a better service level."

We've all heard the adage "the customer is always right." Unfortunately, not all businesses, whether large or small, actually take that truism to heart. The marketplace is littered with the corpses of companies who chose to ignore that adage, yet many small businesses persist in disregarding it. Don't make the mistake of thinking the truth doesn't apply to you. You're NOT an exception to the rule.

"When companies lose track of who their customers are and what their customers mean to them, and they begin to think there's something unique and special about them or their product, they are cruising for a bruising," says marketing guru Shereshewsky.

■ ■ ■ ■ ■ ■

What every customer needs is someone who gives a damn about solving their problem.
—Paul Orfalea, founder, Kinko's

■ ■ ■ ■ ■ ■ ■

Small businesses can be very good at handling customers in a way that their big competitors can't, adds entrepreneur and marketing expert Rogers. "In doing that, they are remembering things for the customer, anticipating what a customer might want next, and are servicing customers in ways that really make sense for those customers."

When Zane started his business, he couldn't compete directly with his rivals on price or inventory because he was so small, he says. "So we built from Day One the fact that we were going to be different based on having a customer relationship that was built on lifetime value versus one built on a transaction. From Day One we also focused on growing the business by working with individual customers and supplying all their needs," says Zane.

■ ■ ■ ■ ■ ■ ■ ■

It's mind share, not market share. We want to be at the top of everyone's mind. When you think of a bike shop in New Haven County, Connecticut, I haven't done my job if that's not us.
—Chris Zane, Zane's Cycles

■ ■ ■ ■ ■ ■ ■ ■

When Walmart announced it was moving next door, literally, Zane didn't panic. He realized, instead, that he needed to bump up his service offerings and to lock in relationships with his customers so they wouldn't see Walmart as an equal alternative. Zane's now-famous lifetime free service policy was born. Other innovative service policies include bicycle trade-in program for kids' bikes, and lifetime parts warranties. "All these things built up our relationships with our customers so that if they went elsewhere, they faced tremendous switching costs," says Zane.

Choose your battles

That doesn't mean you should compromise your ethics, product quality, or fiscal soundness to please or appease your customers. But it does mean that you had better be selective in picking your battles. If a customer is dissatisfied for whatever reason—whether it's with your product, service, or staff, or something else entirely—work with the customer to resolve the problem. Don't simply ignore the problem or walk away.

When the disgruntled advertiser we mentioned earlier threatened libel, I didn't simply decide I was right and he was wrong and hand him off to our attorney. I called the attorney, but I also painstakingly worked for weeks with the unhappy customer to try to resolve the problem to his satisfaction without compromising our ethics. A libel lawsuit, no matter its outcome, is *not* good for our brand.

Beware your reputation

You must always manage your reputation. Whether or not a business or individual buys something from you or your company, take care of everyone as if they were your best customer, says Holstein. Several years ago, a business came to then-fledgling CableOrganizer.com with what amounted to a $70,000 purchase. Holstein considered what might happen to his business if the company were unable to pay or some other unfortunate scenario unfolded, but he gambled on the risk and decided to go for the cash.

"We took the $70,000 sale, and everything went wrong," says Holstein. "The product was delayed, and when it was finally delivered, it had been manufactured incorrectly. We ended up losing our butts on the deal. But the important thing is we took care of the customer. We put 100 percent into doing the right thing, and took care of them all the way. At least they didn't go out and tell everyone how bad we were, and there were no negative Web blog posts."

■ ■ ■ ■ ■ ■

If you want to run a business with longevity, with legs and future equity in the form of long-term and repeating clients and customers, you have to service those clients and customers with a maniacal zeal. Otherwise you'll end up flipping assets or, worse, without assets.

—Harvey Mackay

■ ■ ■ ■ ■ ■

When Aloha Airlines announced its bankruptcy in 2008, GreatHawaiiVacations.com was left with scores of customers whose vacation dreams (and the cost of those airline tickets) were dashed. Instead of shrugging her shoulders and saying, "It's not our fault, and we can't do anything about it," co-owner Goldberg, her husband, and their staff scrambled to help those customers find alternative transportation to Hawaii and back.

That quick and helpful reaction to their customers' needs was just one more reflection of the way the Goldbergs do business. Their methodology has made an impression on their business-to-business suppliers, too, says Goldberg. Those huge B2B suppliers recognize that not only does the staff know its product—Hawaii—cold, but that GreatHawaiiVacations.com's priority is to take care of the client, no matter what. That knowledge and commitment draws a huge repeat clientele.

"These companies say up front that normally they would never give the kind of contract they give to us to a company our size," says Goldberg. "But they tell us we get those contracts because of what we bring to the table and the kind of people we are, because we emanate the spirit and morals that come from our heart."

Customer contact counts

Don't lose sight of the fact that the most important person(s) in your company is the individual(s) with direct customer contact. As Tattered Cover's Meskis indicated in Chapter 3, she's the face of Tattered Cover, but her employees are the connection to the customers.

If, for example, you're an overnight delivery service, the CEO isn't the primary representative of your company and its brand. Your front-line representative is the deliveryman, the person with direct customer contact. If he or she is prompt, efficient, and friendly, that's the reputation of your product—in this case, overnight delivery.

In the absence of direct person-to-person contact, the product itself carries the brand and controls the instant gratification (or lack of) associated with it.

If our customers receive their business journals and the ink is smeared and blurry, they don't care if it was a press malfunction or if I scribbled on every issue. All they know is that the product isn't up to standards, it doesn't measure up to the brand, and we must provide adequate compensation, monetary or otherwise, to make up for it.

The changing face of service

Service isn't static, either. Just as products evolve, so does service, says Mackay. "If customers expect you to present your total product and service offering on the Internet, for example, you better be there...and be present in the latest, fully interactive way," he says. If you're not, plenty of your competitors are.

Remember some of the online fiascos of the 1990s? It seemed as if every company—Big Box or not—jumped on the e-bandwagon with high hopes and dollar signs in their eyes. But few researched the medium enough upfront to recognize the right way to set up a successful interactive Website. The result: plenty of famous fiascos the first time around. eBags, however, took its time, did it right, and from those early days still thrives today. Thousands more Websites and their businesses fell by the wayside. Even Big Box types choked and were forced to regroup their e-forces, heading back to the drawing board to find a better approach.

Check out the competition

How does your company's customer service stack up to your competition's? You had better know, and then make sure you equal and surpass it! How do you find out? Call your customer service desk as a customer/client and find out. Call your competitors, too. And do it sooner rather than later, or you could find yourself playing catch-up in a game that won't wait.

Be careful when outsourcing your customer service, too. Your representatives—the outsourcers—absolutely must be familiar with and informed about the nuances of your product or service. Goldberg offers an amusing—albeit sad—example of what happens when a Big Box outsources offshore. It's also a reflection of how easy it is to compete with and surpass Big Box competition with customer service done right. Says Goldberg:

> Occasionally we will call our competition to check their customer service and see how their agents respond. Recently we called one major company with a request for a beachfront room at a particular hotel we know on Maui. The call was transferred to an offshore outsource facility. We already know there's no such thing as a beachfront room at this particular hotel because it's across the street from the beach and at best offers only a partial peek at the water. But, we ask the agent anyway, to see if he knows his product. The agent, however, responded, "Our oceanfront rooms are sold out. But I have a very nice partial ocean view."

Still not convinced this kind of outsourcing doesn't work? Goldberg recounts another tale. She and her husband called another competitor that also outsources customer service and asked how the beaches differ between two hotels on Maui. The agent's response: "How do you spell 'Maui'?"

"But our people could tell you in a flash how the beach is different because we've all put our feet in the water," says Goldberg. "What sets us apart is we know Hawaii." Her company takes its niche and its employee training very seriously, and it shows in its product and repeat business.

The golden (sales) rules

Do unto others as you would have them do unto you. "If you treat your customers, your business associates, and your suppliers the way you would like to be treated, you will win. If you give them the service that you would expect and want, you will win. If you put them first as you would have them put you first, you will win," says Shereshewsky. "It's really that dumb and simple. That's it. There are all sorts of tricks to the game, but that's the fundamental rule. If you like getting birthday cards, send birthday cards; you'll get birthday cards. Do you like it when people treat you nice? Treat them nice. They'll treat you nice back. It's not hard. We make it hard."

Craigslist.org's founder Newmark agrees. "We all seem to share the value of treating people like you want to be treated. The idea (in this business) is to follow through," says Newmark, who specializes in customer service. "If you are going to follow through with that shared value, you must get serious about customer service."

■ ■ ■ ■ ■ ■ ■

Customer Service Made Easy

- ■ Get to know your customers.
- ■ Treat your customers as you would like to be treated.
- ■ Be responsive to your customers' needs, always!
- ■ Don't compromise your ethics, but negotiate to solve problems.
- ■ Avoid lawsuits.
- ■ Listen to what your customers say.
- ■ Do better every day.

■ ■ ■ ■ ■ ■ ■ ■

For Newmark and his company, that means being responsive to customer issues, comments, and complaints—and in a timely manner. "The only time during business hours you don't hear from me after a couple of hours is if I am on a plane or in a sensitive business meeting," Newmark says.

CableOrganizer.com's competitors are the big electrical suppliers. These larger firms present their own customer service issues that, as a small business, Holstein's company must compete against. Because the competition doesn't answer customer calls or give out quotes over the phone, answering the phone promptly and readily giving out product quotes are standard operating procedures at CableOrganizer.com.

"We don't have to be great. We just have to be better than the competition," says Holstein. "We don't have to set the bar so high that we can't achieve it. We just try to improve and do better every day. And guess what? If you do it right, you will do well."

Generating Sales

To boost your bottom line, boost your sales. It's as easy as that. Remember Sam Hishmeh's mantra to build sales:

1. Don't lose any customers.

2. Get new customers.

"It doesn't get any simpler than that," he says.

Of course, actually following through to gain new customers while keeping your current ones requires strategizing and hard work.

■ ■ ■ ■ ■ ■

Smart people spell service SERVE US.

—Harvey Mackay, author, speaker, entrepreneur

■ ■ ■ ■ ■ ■

Entrepreneurs rarely start out with the expertise they need in sales. It takes more than some "experience" selling retail behind a counter as a teen to be an expert. Even promoting a product or working with a marketing department may not be enough to truly understand the ins and outs of the sales business. We found that out with the *Pacific Coast Business Times*. I panicked unnecessarily when we launched the paper because I was desperate for circulation. If I had paid more attention to ad sales early on, I'd have realized that revenues from target marketing of advertising space would more than make up for any circulation weaknesses, and that, as ad sales picked up, so would circulation. Hindsight is great in business. Just be sure you, too, learn from your mistakes!

Creating the right environment

In today's tough economic environment complicated by Big Box competition everywhere, it's especially important that a small business create a positive sales environment—a corporate environment that's encouraging and rewarding for your salespeople to sell, your staff to service, and your customers to buy.

■ ■ ■ ■ ■ ■ ■ ■

If being fair to customers sets up a conflict with your company's financial goals, then your business model is broken.

—Don Peppers and Martha Rogers, authors, *Rules to Break & Laws to Follow*

■ ■ ■ ■ ■ ■ ■

Mackay, author of *Swim with the Sharks Without Being Eaten Alive: Outsell, Outmanage, Outmotivate, and Outnegotiate Your Competition* (Collins Business Essentials, 2005), has a few suggestions on how to do that:

- Position yourself as a consultant to your customer. Give that customer intelligence about the marketplace. Study your customer's challenges and your ***customer's*** customer.

- Come up with meaningful solutions to the customer's tough problems. The mark of a good salesperson is that his or her customer doesn't regard him or her as a salesperson at all, but as a trusted and indispensable adviser—an auxiliary employee who, fortunately, is on someone else's payroll.

■ Beware cutting your sales staff. Before you cut back your sales or marketing staff, have you calculated the *contribution* to overhead you might be throwing out the window?

■ When times are tough, companies need to do some belt-tightening. However, the one area I wouldn't cut is sales. Andrew Carnegie once said, "You can take away all my money and all my factories, but leave me my sales force and I will be back where I am today in two years." A downturn is no time to sell yourself short.

Renowned speaker, author, and sales expert Alan J. Parisse offers a few more suggestions to ensure sales success. "Sell yourself first. All salespeople get objections, but salespeople with doubts and concerns get a lot more objections," says Parisse. "As the owner/operator of the small business your role is essential and critical to sales. Without you, it won't work. That doesn't mean you have to be a salesperson. It does mean that you must fully appreciate that sales and marketing are not simply necessary evils. Try this quick test: When the chips are down in your business and tough decisions have to be made, who is in the room? If it's all sales and marketing, that can be a problem. But if those functions are excluded or brought in as an afterthought, any solution is likely NOT to work, either," adds Parisse. "Let's say the boss is a technical genius. It easily could be counterproductive for that boss to try to be the primary salesperson. However, a much smarter approach is for him or her to bring in top salespeople, lend support to them, and honor their role. Then they will create or reinforce the boss's image as a technological genius."

Focus on strategic customers

Your customers are your assets. Focus on them, manage them, and handle them with care. That's what customer relationship management is all about. For some businesses, such as mine, that depend on a number of large contracts, focusing on the strategic customers who give us those contracts makes sense. For other businesses that rely on many small contracts or sales, such as Zane's Cycles, every single customer makes a difference.

"The way we go to market, it's putting ourselves in the mind of the consumer versus putting ourselves in the mindset of what works for us. We can figure out how to be profitable once we know what the consumer wants, and then we just manage it. We build it from 'Z' to 'A' instead of 'A' to 'Z,'" says Zane.

■ ■ ■ ■ ■ ■ ■

Because your customers communicate with other customers, the experience you give them is more important than the message.

—Don Peppers and Martha Rogers

■ ■ ■ ■ ■ ■ ■

As a business owner, you should periodically sit down and assess just who those strategic customers are.

From the Trenches

We at the *Pacific Coast Business Times have* learned that even at our small company, it's vitally important to align our relations with customers correctly when we do business with large companies. CEOs and top executives want to interact with me not only because I am the owner, but also because I'm the guy who's running the news team and has my pulse on the economy and what that CEO's competitors are doing. That is valuable information.

Meanwhile, our publisher, George Wolverton, is the person who can work with a senior vice president of marketing to understand an advertiser's strategy and map out a plan. Our account executives interact with schedulers or ad agency personnel to get the timing right on when an ad should run, and to make sure the artwork for that ad is right, too.

If we are all in the right roles, things work great. But if the roles start to get mixed up, communications get very dicey up and down the line, and we run into problems. We learned that lesson the hard way in the early days of the *Business Times* when we could not afford our own production equipment and used our printer's computers to produce the newspaper. The arrangement worked fine for editorial content, but if an advertiser sent us an ad change during the week, the technicians at our printer often didn't get the message, and the wrong ad ended up in the newspaper.

When we went to in-house production in late 2002, we hired our own full-time graphics person to deal with ad changes, and that kind of quality issue pretty much disappeared overnight.

Sales wizard Parisse offers some words of caution, however, when it comes to a business owner focusing on strategic customers. "Depending on the nature of your business and your customer base, clearly it makes sense to focus on your 'A Book.' But be careful. *Relegating* as opposed to *delegating* the 'little people' to the staff sends a message to those other customers that they aren't valuable," says Parisse.

Once again, it's about paying attention to the details. As we talked about earlier, focusing on or counting too much on one single strategic customer can cause problems, too. Think about the $70,000 single-customer deal that went awry for the then-fledgling CableOrganizer.com.

Controlling Your Growth

Whether you're launching a small business or struggling to make an existing one succeed, possibly the furthest thing from your mind is a plan to handle overwhelming success and expansion. I know I certainly didn't worry much about it in those early days, but I should have. That's exactly the time that you as an entrepreneur need to set your business goals and plans for growth and development so that, if and when you achieve it, you're not without direction. Growth must be controlled so it doesn't end up controlling you—and your life.

You probably know someone—if not yourself!—who owns and operates a small business and whose life is consumed by that business. That person works 24/7 and has no time for himself or their family. Entrepreneurship shouldn't be that way, and it doesn't have to be if you've planned properly.

Each of us can probably think of at least one very successful small business—perhaps a restaurant or retail establishment—that had a great concept, tons of loyal customers, and a hardworking owner whom everyone knew and liked. The company probably did so well that the owner decided to expand to a second, third, or maybe even fourth location. However, unless that small-business owner grew his business in a controlled and methodical way with an emphasis on quality control and a well-run management group, chances are that the expansion wasn't nearly as successful as expected, and maybe even fell flat.

I recall one such restaurant in downtown Denver. Despite all the competition, it was standing room only at all but the most obscure times. The food was excellent; the service impeccable; and you actually looked forward to saying hi to the owner, who always seemed to be there to meet, greet, and make sure his restaurant and its product were flawless. It wasn't a high-end restaurant. On the contrary, it was casual, borderline tacky décor, and reasonably priced, but the food was the best and the owner made it all work perfectly. Expansion was natural, and its success in any location a foregone conclusion. Not so fast, though.

The owner chose a location far away from his existing restaurant—from downtown to a rural suburb where "eatertainment" was the norm, prices mattered less, and tacky décor was a definite liability. He had neither a reliable management team nor a good quality-control system in place, and was stretched way too thin to make the expansion work. You can guess the rest. After only a short time, the suburban location folded for lack of customers and interest. Luckily, the business' owner was able to return to his roots—the downtown restaurant—and at last count it was still going strong.

Don't let your business fall into the same syndrome. Approach growth as part of your overall business plan. How will you handle it? Set goals, and outline the groundwork for expansion when those goals are achieved. Before Domino's Hishmeh bought more franchise outlets, he made sure he had a handle on the system, growth, and quality control. He had a family-based management team he could count on, and he knew he could grow and gain rather than grow and lose.

To be a success, you don't have to set your sights on becoming a Fortune 500 company, but you do have to recognize what it is you want and how you will handle that success if and when you achieve it.

Sorting Through the Sales Clutter

Google the words *small business*, *generate*, and *sales*, and you get literally millions of entries peppered with words such as *high velocity*, *inexpensive*, *easy*, *successful*, and more. Thousands of books have been written about selling and mulevel marketing, too, and almost everyone in business has his or her version of a successful sales approach. You can tune the TV to sales gurus and selling hype anytime day or night.

Do you listen or do you tune it all out? I find that listening objectively to the talk can be, if nothing else, a good indicator of what not to do. There's plenty of hype out there, especially on the Internet, and it's simply that: hype, as in multilevel marketing schemes to get your money. Save the cash, and pick up some good books on selling from your public library instead.

Use your common sense when it comes to sorting through the sales clutter, says Parisse, also a nationally known speaker specializing in "Thriving in Turbulent Times." The Boulder, Colorado–based Parisse was named by *Successful Meetings* magazine as one of the "Top 21 Speakers for the 21st Century" and has been elected to the Speakers Hall of Fame. Keep in mind, too, says Parisse, what F.W. Woolworth, entrepreneur and founder of F.W. Woolworth stores, once said: "I am the world's worst salesman, therefore, I must make it easy for people to buy."

Your Ammunition

Some essentials to remember from this chapter include:

- Take the time to get to know your customers. Learn about them, and it will pay big dividends in terms of sales.

- Your customers are your assets. Without them and without sales, you don't have a business. Remember that.

- Do check on your company's customer service. Call your service or front desk to discover how your staff reacts. If their response isn't up to standards, find out why not, and work with your employees to change it. It also helps to have written expectations and a system in place to measure those expectations.

- Check out the competition's service and help desks, too. Make sure your company's service and help surpasses the competition's.

CHAPTER
6

GET A GRIP ON CASH: FINANCIAL MANAGEMENT

What you find in small companies is not that they have bad budgeting. They usually have none.
—Peter Iannone, director, CBIZ/MHM (an acounting, tax, and advisory services firm, Los Angeles)

For too many small businesses, dollars and cents don't always make sense. But they can and should if—as the business's owner/operator—you take the commonsense approach. Enthusiasm and a good idea simply aren't enough for long-term success. The numbers must add up, too.

"The entrepreneurial spirit is only one element. You have to be able to manage the financial aspect, too, and that's tough. There are a billion good ideas in this world," says Tattered Cover Book Store's Joyce Meskis.

That doesn't mean a business owner also needs to be an economist, a math wizard, or a number-cruncher. But you better have a business plan and an understanding of your cost structures and more if you intend to succeed.

"You don't need to personally have the expertise. But you need to recognize that you must get that expertise," says entrepreneur Shereshewsky. For one thing, you must be able to recognize if there's enough cash in the till to meet your bills. That sounds elementary, but you might be surprised at the number of small (and large) businesses that just don't get it."

"In the long run, everything relates to finance," says Peter Iannone, director of CBIZ/MHM, an accounting, tax, and advisory services firm in Los Angeles, California. The company (NYSE: CBZ; *www.cbiz.com*), based in Cleveland, Ohio, provides professional support, consultants, and services to businesses on issues ranging from accounting and taxes to benefits and insurance.

Plenty of sources, from community colleges to universities, schools, industry and professional organizations, books, magazines, the Web, and myriad consultants, and other options, are available to help you learn what you need to know.

■ ■ ■ ■ ■ ■ ■ ■ ■

Starting Points for Financial Information

Small-business people can find help with financial needs from a variety of sources—some free or low cost. Here's a sampling of only a few:

■ Business Owner's Toolkit (*www.toolkit.com*)
■ Disney Entrepreneur Center (*www.disneyec.com*)
■ Ewing Marion Kauffman Foundation (*www.kauffman.org*)
■ Inc. (*www.inc.com*)
■ Internal Revenue Service (*www.irs.gov/businesses/small*)
■ MyMoney.gov (*www.mymoney.gov*)
■ New York City Small Business Research Center (*www.nypl.org/research/sibl/smallbiz/sbrc/Pages/index.cfm*)

- NFIB from the National Federation of Independent Business (*www.NFIB.com*)
- Small Business Online Community from Bank of America (*http://smallbusinessonlinecommunity.bankofamerica.com/index.jspa*)
- SmartBiz (*www.smartbiz.com*)
- U.S. Small Business Administration (*www.sba.gov*)
- 360 Degrees of Financial Literacy from the American Society of Certified Public Accountants (*www.360financialliteracy; www.aicpa.org*)
- Wells Fargo Small Business (*www.wellsfargo.com/biz*)

Business Finance 101

Rule number one, according to CableOrganizer.com's Holstein, is quite simple: If your business doesn't have the money to do something, don't do it. If, for example, you need more staff but can't afford the expense of additional full-time employees, consider other options such as contract or part-time workers. Never add employees you can't afford, says Holstein, a CPA by trade.

Unfortunately, planning and staff management aren't always given the attention they require. Holstein singles out Ford Motor Company as an example. How, on May 31st, could the automaker have a purpose for some 4,000 employees, only to lose the need for them on June 1st and lay off the entire group? Such downsizing generally occurs because of a management failure, he says. "If companies looked at their needs every day instead of every five years, they'd have far fewer layoffs," he adds.

Your Business Plan

Turning an entrepreneurial dream into successful economic reality starts with a business plan, which is a long-range document that outlines your business strategies and more. If success is on

your agenda, you'd better believe that. Plenty of people don't see
the need for a business plan, and their failed businesses have van-
ished from industries of every stripe. That's especially true in today's
challenging economic climate. "Times of economic downturn often showcase the resiliency of small-business owners," says Rebecca
Macieira-Kaufmann, former head of the Wells Fargo & Company's
small business segment. The bank is one of the nation's major
lenders to small business. "What's critical now, as in any economic
environment, is that business owners maintain strong financial
management practices and plan for the future," she adds.

"I've heard stories about how people with wonderful vision
and ideas go into business without a business plan. I cannot imagine that," says Meskis. "The counsel I'd offer to would-be entrepreneurs is perseverance. Take the time to really work out the details.
A colleague who used to teach booksellers always said, 'Sweat the
details.' That's what it is about—detail, detail, detail—in all aspects of business."

As a business owner, you must have a plan and understand
what's involved financially to achieve your goals, agrees
Shereshewsky. Master framer Del Spina, for example, developed a
detailed plan of operation showing his business's path to profitability *before* his first customer ever walked through the door of his
showroom/retail store. With the plan in place, he acquired a long-
term lease, built out his store to look terrific, and bought materials
and goods for his business. Only then did he open his store.

At the *Pacific Coast Business Times*, even though we purchased
an existing small newspaper, we still had to design a business plan,
find and lease suitable office space, purchase equipment, negotiate
vendor contracts, hire and pay staff, and position ourselves to succeed before we ever put out our first edition. (See Addendum B for
a sample of what to include in your business plan.)

Without proper planning and the right financial preparation/
backing, such expenses can doom a company. Plan wisely and with
profits in mind whether you're opening a new business or retrofitting

an older one. That's especially important in today's rocky economy. "The single biggest mistake that people leading small businesses make is they don't create a clear plan and then stick with it," adds career coach and author McKee. "Then when times get tough, they don't have a clear direction to work towards, and mistakes and confusion results."

Says Iannone: "Someone mentoring me in my career once said, 'You have to know where you are going. Otherwise you are just wandering all over the map trying to get to somewhere. You could pass right by it, but you didn't know where you were going so how would you know whether you got there?' Your strategic plan is where you are going."

Elements of your business plan should include:

- Clearly defined goals and a time line to achieve those goals.

- A blueprint of how much money you will need and how you will spend that money.

- Reasonable salaries for yourself and others. If, for example, this is your first startup and you have a big ownership stake, $75,000 per year might be fair. As we've mentioned previously, however, you may have to forgo that salary or take much less to ensure your business's profitability.

- A description of the market niche you hope to occupy and a brief description of each of your competitors, actual or potential.

- Descriptions of the key people involved in the project, the idea being to prove your team has the competence to get the job done.

- A budget template for the first 18 to 24 months; make sure the numbers actually add up.

And don't think that because you do have a business plan, the planning stops there. Far from it. Successful businesses require realistic and ongoing planning, says Ask Alice's Magos. In fact, failure to plan is the biggest mistake small businesses make, she adds.

Keep in mind, too, that strategic direction, even in small companies, takes time to come to fruition and show promise, adds Iannone. That's as compared with tactical plans, which are shorter term and spell out day to day, week to week, and month to month exactly what must be done to achieve your strategic goals.

Right-designing for profitability

A small business absolutely must be designed for profitability, says veteran entrepreneur and advertising executive Cathey M. Finlon in Denver, Colorado.

When I started in small business, I came out of a non-profit background and didn't totally understand growth. Further, I didn't understand that a business had to be profitable. I thought break-even would be good enough," says Finlon. "I didn't realize that if you want to be in business for a long time, you need to make a profit and you need to think about growth. Staying small works, but you might not be able to hang onto the same people the whole time because, without growth, they don't have a career path and they don't have salary increases.

Many people in the early stages of a business don't think they have to fund themselves that way," she adds. "But you don't have a business until you've sold a product and until you've made a profit. That reality is sometimes difficult for people who are starting a small business to understand.

■ ■ ■ ■ ■ ■ ■ ■

If you have a business and you don't have any customers (sales), you don't really have a business; you have a hobby. That's probably the most important No. 1 thing for a small business to remember.
—Martha Rogers, Peppers & Rogers Group

■ ■ ■ ■ ■ ■ ■ ■

Think it through up front

Whatever your business, you must design its structure and size to be profitable, period. If your pathway to profitability requires investors, then you need those investors before you actually start. If it doesn't require investors and can be bootstrapped, do so in a way that allows the business to start out with a profit. That could mean not paying yourself until the business IS profitable, Finlon adds.

Jon Nordmark and his eBags, Sam Hishmeh and his Domino's Pizza franchises, and many others (including me!) know what it's like to forgo a salary while getting a business off the ground.

Spaced out

A concrete aspect of designing for profitability includes purchasing or leasing the ideal (read that affordable) physical space from which to operate your business. For CableOrganizer.com, a bootstrapped operation, Holstein's garage initially doubled as workspace to conserve the company's limited capital. For master picture framer Thomas Del Spina, an historic, refurbished warehouse doubled as retail space and showroom for his manufactured product—specialized picture frames. If you're seeking profitability, design for it—even if your business isn't a start up.

Small businesses also must pay attention to whether their sales volume justifies the cost of rent for their facility, adds Del Spina. Typically that means figuring how much in product or services you must sell per square foot of office or retail space to justify the cost of that space. The rule of thumb, says Del Spina, is to multiply your monthly rent or payment times 10 to determine the amount of goods or services you need to sell.

"My monthly rent, for example, is $4,000. That means I have to sell $40,000 of product every month to justify my rent," says Del Spina. (That's doable given the volume of his business and the high price point of his products.) "Can you imagine a vacuum cleaner store with $7,000 a month rent? How many vacuums would that person have to sell to justify his rent?" Plenty, no doubt!

Of course, that's only one aspect of the planning, figuring, and processing that goes into designing for profitability. Nonetheless, it can make or break a company.

Del Spina's hypothetical vacuum store has its real-life counterpart. A photography studio in metropolitan Denver appeared to be extremely successful. (We won't name the company out of deference to its owners' privacy.) Although they weren't big names, its photographers did a good job. A chunk of the studio's business came from shooting senior high school pictures, and the well-appointed studio was always busy. Appointments for photo sittings had to be made well in advance, and everything seemed to be going quite well—except for one problem. The company's owner had opted to lease very visible and very costly space. Rent was $5,600 a month.

The studio's rates were far from cheap, but imagine how many pictures two photographers would have to take to generate 10 times the $5,600 a month rent at an average $300 to $500 per customer. Most likely hundreds. As you can surmise, it was an uphill battle, and eventually the studio closed, in part because its owner simply didn't understand the necessity of designing for profitability.

The equipment issue

Don't assume that purchasing all the equipment you need for your business makes the most economic sense, either. It depends. We purchased our equipment because we've always believed in financing the company with cash and avoiding any sort of debt, except for occasional working capital loans to fund payroll when receivables are high and cash short. Also, at the time it was tough for us as a start-up with no credit history to get a lease or any other financing. Instead, then and now, we take advantage of any "same as cash" deals to buy computers and other equipment to string out our payments and not run up interest costs. We also use a corporate charge card for certain equipment purchases such as computers, and always pay it off within 30 days or use money from our credit line to pay it off and avoid interest charges.

Your business, on the other hand, may opt for another approach. You may be able to find a great deal to lease equipment, which especially makes sense if you're dealing with constantly changing technologies. Also, just as you may opt to outsource an aspect such as payroll or cleaning services, you also might find that outsourcing secretarial, bookkeeping, or even contracting with a virtual (telecommuting or home-based) individual is more cost effective. More and more service companies are turning to the virtual model, too—think the Garrett Planning Network that we talked about in Chapter 3, where their employees work from home, saving thousands of dollars annually on office expenses. The home-based outlet approach is gaining popularity in the retail sector, too, with everything from purses to candles, T-shirts, gifts, and more. In fact, some specialty chain retailers now even advertise in-your-home parties to compete.

There is no absolute right answer to what works best for your business. What is essential, though, is for you as a small-business owner/operator to be open to various options. Consider them, run the numbers, and then decide what works best for you in terms of finances and customer service.

Occasionally, too, you may simply fall into an incredible deal. Our landlord, a local bank, gave us a big break on the lease for our office space for the first year, with payments to accelerate during the next three years. That year passed, but the bank never increased our rent. They apparently forgot about it until year three when suddenly they sent us a bill for $20,000 in back rent!

I nearly fell off my chair. But I quickly regrouped and called the CFO of the bank. We discussed it and eventually reached an agreement. The bank took $5,000 in cash and some of our security deposit, and then rolled the rest of the increase into the balance of the year's lease.

They must have been impressed that we were able to pay because they then offered us a new three-year lease with simple cost-of-living accelerators in the rent.

We accepted. I then spent a long weekend retouching the paint in our office, and the bank provided new carpet, including its installation, for our office. (That was no small freebie considering the old carpet was yellow shag!) As a bonus, they also opened the doors to their surplus furniture warehouse for us to take any desks and chairs that we wanted—free. So, now we have offices packed with cherry wood desks and side chairs with navy blue upholstery. It looks very buttoned-down, but our advertisers and other visitors are impressed.

The over/under dilemma

Many of the problems small businesses face are the result of owners/operators overestimating sales, underestimating costs, or both, says Holstein. Many entrepreneurs live on "Hope Island," the land of eternal optimism, he adds. "They think, 'If I set up this eBiz Website, I'll have tons of business instantly.' That's 'Hope Island.' These business owners don't think they have to work to get the sales," he adds.

Shereshewsky lays the blame for small-business failures often on the fact that they're undercapitalized and have cost structures incompatible with the business they're in. For example, restaurants open and close frequently because they tend to be opened by people without the necessary experience. They pay too much for real estate and equipment, or they don't understand how to negotiate the best deals with their suppliers. Ultimately, they find themselves in situations where it's obvious they haven't considered the fundamental issues of being in business, says Shereshewsky.

Cash Concerns

One of the fundamentals of business is to know the difference between cash and revenues. Revenues do not equal cash. Those figures on your financial statement don't equal what's in your checking account, either, because of irritating details such as depreciation, accrued expenses, and more. What's worse, your business's checking account may be flush right now, but what about the deluge of bills due BEFORE you're likely to get another shot in the arm of revenue? Don't be discouraged if that's your business's modus operandi. You're not alone. These are very real issues faced by all businesses, especially those with products or services that go out the door before the paycheck comes in. It's your job as the business's owner/operator to keep track of the cash—on a daily, weekly, monthly, and annual basis.

Be careful, too, not to lose sight of the fact that the $30,000 in your checking account on Monday doesn't go very far if $15,000 rent is due on Friday and you're $45,000 in arrears to your biggest supplier.

You can, however, lessen your chances of coming up short when it comes to meeting those financial obligations in a timely manner. Let's take a closer look at how some successful small businesses handle the conundrum of cash.

Working capital

Working capital is the cash—or fast access to it—that you as a business's owner/operator have on hand to use at any given time. It's something many small businesses, start-ups or not, often run short of.

That lack of access to working capital is the single biggest challenge small-business owners face today, says Business Toolkit's Magos. Small-business owners absolutely must pay attention to precise and constant cash-flow planning, inventory micromanagement, and aggressive receivable collections to overcome the cash dilemma, she adds.

"Entrepreneurs fall into the cash flow trap because they are optimistic by nature. If they weren't, they wouldn't be starting a business," says John J. Huggins, successful entrepreneur, angel investor, and member of the board of directors of the *Pacific Coast Business Times*. He's also my chief business confidant/advisor. Huggins experienced his own entrepreneurial success as former

CFO of Johnson-Grace Company, a start-up he co-founded in 1992 with two friends from graduate school. The company developed a streaming media commercial application that allowed a computer file to be played or used before it was fully downloaded. In 1996, they sold the company to America Online for $85 million in stock in that company.

Unfortunately, a common mistake small-business owners make, especially with start-ups, is to underestimate how much working capital they'll need, says Huggins. "Entrepreneurs need to maintain their optimism, but they also need to be deliberately cautious or pessimistic when estimating their working capital needs," he says. "That means you optimistically estimate what your working capital needs are, and then you double or triple it!"

Even if you think you have enough working capital, you easily can come up short.

"Start-ups can fairly well estimate the cost of the material things such as office space and computers. But they often raise only that amount, or not even that amount, and then open for business. They fail to plan for the fact that it takes time to build up their accounts payable and that businesses, even big businesses, take a long time to pay," Huggins says.

That's what happened at the *Pacific Coast Business Times*. "Henry struggled with this in the beginning, not so much because we didn't plan for it, but because we underestimated how long it would take to build up revenue," says Huggins. "Once you're in that cycle of never having enough cash, it becomes a major distraction from the job of growing the business. Instead you're trying to figure out how to cover the American Express bill or making sure you have enough cash to meet the payroll. It ends up taking a lot of *management bandwidth* that should be used on actually growing the business," he adds.

■ ■ ■ ■ ■ ■ ■ ■

When determining your company's working capital needs, keep in mind that it's always going to take longer and go more slowly and not be quite as rosy as you think or hope.

—John J. Huggins, successful entrepreneur, angel investor

■ ■ ■ ■ ■ ■ ■ ■

The right amount of working capital for your business depends on your industry and plenty more. But various consulting sources, bankers, industry organizations, and even the SBA have (and generally will share) useful rules of thumb for how much working capital, capital per employee, and more is required for your business.

"I would encourage people to seek out those yardsticks and measure themselves," says Huggins. "They are not strict rules that every business needs to meet. But they do give you a sense of how you compare financially to your peers and can show you—regarding amounts of working capital, for example—where you might be more vulnerable than you think. They also help you understand how someone who may provide financing—whether debt or equity—will look at your business. Even if you don't think a certain rule of thumb applies to your business, it may be the lens an investor is going to view you through, so you might as well know what it is and how it looks."

Cash-flow conundrum

Most companies count on generating cash during a particular time frame, which poses certain problems. An amusement park or golf course, for example, is likely to get most of its cash between Memorial Day and Labor Day. Those businesses must learn how to cope with the relatively cashless remainder of the year. A ski resort, on the other hand, generates its big bucks during the winter ski months, with lighter income from hikers, bikers, and sightseers during the warmer months. A typical retail store looks to the Christmas/holiday-buying season to set the income pace and hopes to break even during the rest of the year. Restaurants generally look to big weekends to bring in the cash, and perhaps a business lunch trade during the week to make ends meet.

Expect complications

Complicating it all, many service companies, including Finlon's advertising agency, have customers who pay all or a portion of cash up front. That's fine, but your business can't spend that cash because it's earmarked for future expenses.

One way around that dilemma and to ensure more consistent cash flow for your business may be to offer customers a price break for buying multiple goods or services and then paying for them on a monthly rather than annual or upfront basis. That's how Tim McGovern, owner of Power Points Inc., handles his cyclical business. McGovern develops and operates football and basketball games for newspapers across the country in which participants pick game winners in exchange for local prizes from the newspapers and grand prizes that his company provides. The professional football season lasts 17 weeks; college bowl games add a few more; and McGovern's third game, Bracket Bucks, addresses the NCAA basketball finals for a few more weeks. The end result is that he has plenty of down time with no money coming in. "I spend half my life in geisha houses (in other words with comfortable amounts of cash coming in) and the other in soup kitchens (no income)," says McGovern.

To ease the financial dry spell, McGovern created his Gold Club for his best clients. "Club" members who sign up for two of his three games get the third free IF they pay over 12 months as opposed to upfront or in a lump sum. "I like it because it spreads out my income," says McGovern, "and my customers like it because they don't have to come up with a big lump-sum payment." There's that win-win collaboration between client and provider again.

Another cash-flow complication: You may never even see 100 percent of the fee for a job if yours is a business that deals with holdbacks, which are a percentage of the fee that's not paid until the job is complete and the client has signed off on the work. In the construction business, for example, the subcontractor or contractor may hold back paying part of the tab until the client signs off on the job. You may do a $900,000 job but not ever see the last $90,000 because of client concerns, so you had better gear your outflow to that upfront figure.

Pay attention to patterns

Whatever your business, you can start with ballpark estimates of your inflow and outflow. Keep in mind, though, that only through time and by trial and error will you uncover the real dollars and cents that govern your business. The key is to pay attention to the numbers and recognize the patterns that develop.

From the Trenches

In early 2002, as we began to make a little cash and our bank and CPA firm began to believe we'd be financially viable, I recognized another vexing problem—how to keep track of the cash. Many companies can be profitable but run into problems if the cash coming in can't meet the payroll or service the debt. In our case, some clients had paid us in cash for a year's worth of ads. That helped meet the payroll in January, but what would we do during the summer doldrums when business was weak and we needed the cash?

Fortunately, I ran into Cathey Finlon, advertising executive, keen observer of cash flow, and owner of McClain-Finlon Advertising, an independent agency in Denver that she had built into a regional powerhouse. Our conversation eventually led to my concern about my company's cash flow. It was hardly a surprise when Cathey said her agency had experienced a similar problem. Clients would pay her a bundle of cash, but then she had to turn around and pay television and radio stations along with newspapers for ads. Those expenditures sometimes depleted her bank account between client payments.

To avoid coming up short, Cathey devised her own one-page worksheet. She sent me a copy, but it was a bit complicated for me. Nonetheless, it became the basis for my own, simpler one-page worksheet that provided the format to operate successfully year-round.

■ ■ ■ ■ ■ ■ ■

Keep Track of Your Cash

A simple worksheet like this can help a small business keep track of cash in any given week. Try rounding your numbers to the nearest $1,000:

Cash-In/Cash-Out
- Checking account balance: $32,000
- Checks and cash received: $20,000
- Check swritten to vendors: $11,000
- Credit card payments: $2,000
- Payroll, including taxes: $23,000
- Closing balance: $16,000

Mini-Financial Snapshot
- Credit line borrowings: $0
- Accounts payable: $30,000
- Credit card charges: $1,000
- Total obligations: $31,000
- Accounts receivable: $130,000
- Closing checking balance: $16,000

■ ■ ■ ■ ■ ■ ■ ■ ■

Payments and collections

The *Pacific Coast Business Times* is a year-round operation; by definition we bring in revenue 12 months of the year, although January is notoriously a weak month. We have our own set of cash woes, however, which are exacerbated by being a business-to-business provider that invoices our customers rather than receiving cash up front as does the ski resort, retailer, restaurant, or the like.

We're the small guy on the block and have learned the hard way that our bigger customers don't pay us in any consistent pattern. Sometimes we receive their check 30 days after an ad appears in the paper; sometimes it takes as long as 120 days. Meanwhile, other companies pay us as soon as we send them an invoice. All this can wreak havoc on the bottom line of any small business unless you're prepared.

As a business's owner/operator, you must figure out the average time a particular client takes to pay. At the *Pacific Coast Business Times*, we receive payment in roughly 40 to 45 days, or about six weeks after we send out an invoice. Therefore, if I look at the total accounts receivable and divide that number by six (as in weeks to payment), I can get a general idea of how much cash inflow to expect in a given week. Of course, you always must allow for some margin of error—six weeks is an average time to payment, which means sometimes longer and sometimes sooner. That's where good credit comes in. We'll talk more about it later, but suffice it to say that with a solid line of credit from the bank—in our case, Wells Fargo—we can borrow enough to make sure the bills get paid and payroll is met if, for some reason, we are short of cash during any given week. Just remember to pay off that line of credit quickly to avoid too many interest payments.

Valuing your product

Money is simply a measure of value, says Finlon. Consequently, how you price your goods or services is a measure of their value. Hard costs aside, small-business owners often have trouble determining the value of their goods or services, standing up for that valuation while helping the customer to appreciate it, and then following through to collect payment in full. Hesitation anywhere along that path can torpedo your ability to charge and collect your fees. If you back down too quickly on a valuation, it looks as if you haven't been truthful, adds Finlon.

If you've honestly valued your product and yet a customer or client balks at the price and says it's not worth it, you must have the gumption either to walk away or help that client understand the value of your goods or services. "If you can't explain the value to a customer, go back to the drawing board, and figure out how to do so," Finlon says.

Controlling your inflow

Although we think small is big, when it comes to collections, small usually takes a backseat to the big guys on the block. That's reality. It's up to you as the owner of your small business to make sure you don't end up short-changed. The right approach early on can help you develop leverage to push your clients to pay more promptly. As "Ask Alice" columnist Magos indicated, aggressive receivables collections are a must to ensure you don't run short of working capital.

"Instead of waiting for someone to pay you, you need to insist on financial terms that will permit your business to succeed," agrees Finlon.

Easier said than done? Maybe, but consider Finlon's approach. She starts by substantiating what she bills her clients, and then they agree on the need for timely payment up front.

"If you know that your inventory—in my case, a service—goes out the door every night, you can't wait for someone to pay you for it six months from now," she says. "You want them to pay you up front, or you want them to pay as you go."

As a small-business owner, you must understand that dynamic, insist on it, and help your customer or client understand why this collaboration—timely payment—between provider and client is advantageous to them. Finlon sees customers and vendors as true financial and business partners. It's important to help them understand that the success of one directly relates to the success of another.

"You're not taking something (cash) from them just so you can have your own way," she says. "You're doing it so you can deliver the service they need in a positive and consistent manner."

Actually, says Finlon, this approach considers the client's best interests. "You're telling the client, 'I can deliver the product or service to you in a timely and consistent way because you've paid me such that I can pay my people so they're motivated to keep doing the work (or producing the product) for you.'"

How does Finlon insist on and ensure this collaboration? She emphasizes that, when a client or customer depends on her business to come through for them, that's a partnering, which requires collaboration. "There must be a common understanding that this kind of collaboration puts everybody in the best possible position to succeed," she adds.

"It's how I pay my vendors," she says. "If I pay them in a timely fashion, I know they will be there for me through thick and thin. Since 1985, when I first started doing this, my goal has been to pay everybody on a 30-day cycle because I wanted them to know that I was in partnership with them. I let them know I understood their needs, and, likewise, they needed to come through for me when I needed them.

"This is where I think small businesses particularly can put a personal face on client relationships. You offer consistency and collaboration and then demonstrate it through payment practice."

Finlon uses the *Pacific Coast Business Times* to illustrate this collaborative approach to timely payment from the client's perspective. It behooves the newspaper's advertisers to be good clients because their goal is to maximize the performance of the newspaper to deliver them the best marketing punch for their advertising dollar. Therefore, says Finlon, it's up to both the *Pacific Coast Business Times* and its client, in this case an advertiser, to communicate clearly to each other the requirements—such as ad content, deadlines, and timely payment—for each of them to achieve their goals.

"Sometimes you have to do business when situations or people aren't that great and it may not be a perfect fit," says Finlon. "But if one is a heat-seeking missile looking for a target or a relationship that is mutual and collaborative so you can build something bigger to achieve a higher aim—wow! Is that ever the most premier position to be in."

■ ■ ■ ■ ■ ■

Why not just adopt a philosophy that says I am going to seek partnerships that work for me, that I really understand, and that I feel I can collaborate with?

—Cathey Finlon   ■ ■ ■ ■ ■ ■

Necessary Financial Disciplines

As a small-business owner, you must learn to handle the money in whatever way necessary so your business survives. That's the bottom line, says Finlon, no matter the business. That goes for inflow and outflow, client payments, and your payments to vendors. In a service business, that could mean insisting on being paid up front before you start or perhaps taking half of the payment up front to enable you to start. If your business is highly seasonal, you may even negotiate with your suppliers to pay over a longer period of time or make lump-sum payments that correspond with your busy months so you don't have to sweat meeting the bills the rest of the year.

Getting revenue and expenses right is only half the battle, however. As we've discussed, the other half is making sure there's enough cash to meet payroll and cover expenses week after week and year after year. To do that takes financial discipline, expertise, and recognizing the importance of separating your money from that of your business. A little luck doesn't hurt, either.

Your money versus business money

Beware a little success and extra cash. It's easy to get an inflated ego, assume an extravagant lifestyle—and be set back a long way.

"Many people in small business get really excited (by their success) and build a giant house and lease a fancy car," says Finlon. "I'm much more a proponent of the middle road. Don't get a big head about the money you make, because just as easy as you got it, it can go away."

Small-business owners must recognize another pitfall, too, says Iannone. Just because they own the business doesn't mean the company's money is their own money to spend freely. If they're really looking out for their own best interests, "There needs to be a separation of church and state, so to speak," he says. "Part of the reasons for wanting to have a small company is the flexibility to be your own boss. But you still need a little bit of separation so you can think strategically and plan for business cycles. Small-business owners tend not to see their business cycles as well as larger, more established companies do."

"I have one client, two partners in a construction company with about $15 million in revenues. They'll have a couple of really good months, and the next thing you know, one of them has a speedboat or their construction crews are working on their houses instead of construction projects. Then they have three bad months and can't figure out where all the money went," adds Iannone.

These owner/operators—just like other small-business people—need to put in place certain financial disciplines to help maintain the separation of business and personal finances, and to plan for the future, too. Larger companies with more diverse ownership already have such disciplines in place, Iannone adds.

The "b" word

An essential financial discipline is a budget. It's a very good tool for even a small company to use, says Iannone, because it helps you think into the future and see that good financial periods will have to carry the business through slower ones if you expect it to survive.

What the budget looks like or how it's compiled isn't as important as putting it together and having the document as a reference point.

"I don't care if the budget is done in Excel or something you've loaded into QuickBooks on your PC. It can even be handwritten," says Iannone. "But there needs to be a document you can refer to that gives you a perspective of your business for a longer time than what's in front of you."

If you don't have a head for business and aren't a number-cruncher or computer geek, consider taking a class or workshop in QuickBooks or Excel before you start on your budget. The budget needn't be complicated, but it should be thorough. In fact, you absolutely don't want the budget to be so complicated and cumbersome that it's never used, says Iannone. Additionally, it should cover one complete business cycle, such as one year, or, in the case of a new business, the period from initial investment to positive cash flow.

At the *Pacific Coast Business Times*, the annual budget is fairly detailed by cost category for revenue and expenses. Additionally, on a weekly basis—actually, every Thursday—our part-time bookkeeper (who works in the office two mornings a week to write checks and make collections calls, and works the rest of her hours at home) provides a report with only four lines:

- Cash deposited.
- Checks paid.
- Total accounts receivable.
- Total accounts payable.

These four numbers tell us if the company has generated enough cash during the week to pay the bills and have enough left over to meet roughly half the payroll. (We pay twice a month.) From the ratio of accounts receivable to accounts payable, we can tell if the future likely will generate enough cash to continue operating without using our credit line. A ratio of at least 2 to 1 usually will do the trick. (For example, accounts receivable of $120,000 versus accounts payable of $60,000.)

From the Trenches

The budget at the *Pacific Coast Business Times* is a WORKING document. That means we don't just draw it up and shove it into a drawer. We're constantly using it, updating it, and referring to it.

I draw up our preliminary budget in the fall for the following year, print it out, and put it in my briefcase so that it goes with me almost everywhere I go. I make small adjustments here and there, mainly when I'm on an airplane and bored out of my skull.

In January, when we know how the year is shaping up, I update the budget across the board, fine-tuning printing costs, mailing costs, personnel expenses, and the cost of healthcare so they're relatively accurate. I then have a very good idea of our "nut" or break-even point.

George Wolverton, our publisher, then goes over the revenue numbers and we reach an agreement on a profit goal, which then becomes part of the budget document. I print out the budget again, and again stash the copy in my ever-traveling briefcase. (The document gets updates in pencil to show variations from the original numbers throughout the year.)

By March, we have a more accurate picture of how the year's numbers will play out. That still leaves us plenty of time to make any necessary adjustments.

By the end of the year, the budget is a bit dog-eared and filled with pencil scratches, but it's usually right on when it comes to expenses. It is, though, I admit, a little optimistic on revenue. Still, we often finish the year pretty close to my original estimates.

Your credit line

The credit line—your business's ability to access quick cash up to a set ceiling—can be a great tool if revenues come up short one month. A credit line also can be a fail-safe backup for a payroll account in case of a slight miscalculation or if you didn't transfer quite enough cash to your company's payroll account. That's happened once at the *Pacific Coast Business Times*. The cost of the backup is minimal and certainly well worth it to avoid the headache and hassle should the account fall short.

A more sophisticated option to a line of credit is short-term financing against receivables, says Iannone. This tends to be good for growing companies or ones with variability in their accounts receivable, because the line grows and shrinks with them as opposed to an ordinary line of credit, which is a static number.

One big caution, though, when it comes to borrowing: If you borrow to smooth out your cash flow, run through the numbers to make sure your business's profitability supports the cost of borrowing, Iannone adds. "You will pay in current terms probably about 7 to 8 percent (interest) on an annualized basis. So if your overall profit margin is 4 percent, a loan may very well take away all or a good portion of it."

Take advantage of trade terms

Pay your bills, says Zane, and your vendors may offer you special deals. Depending on your business, a special deal could be excess inventory offered at a discount, lower prices, favorable terms, and more. Better still, pay your bills early and take all the *anticipation*. That's the interest payments that would have been due. "If there is an opportunity to save a point or 1 percent a month on your cost of goods, if you amortize that over 12 months you get huge discounts off the inventory that you're buying. Managing your money, paying your bills, understanding inventory terms— those are all really important. If you look at the people that are competing in the marketplace today who don't understand that, they go away pretty quickly," says Zane.

With retailers such as Zane's Cycles, for example, it's not necessarily how quick you can turn (sell) inventory, but the financial terms the manufacturer gives you to pay for that inventory that count, says Zane. If we buy one bike for $100 and it takes one year to sell that bike, we've made profit on the $100 once. But if we can get four, five, or six turns of inventory out of that same $100, we've made profit on that $100 four, five, or six times. "Your return on invested capital is exponentially higher if you understand how to get inventory turns and how to buy right, manage inventory, and talk to your vendors," adds Zane.

"In our business, I have almost zero capital invested because I have almost as much inventory as money I owe my vendors. At the end of the day I have no dollars of my own invested in my inventory. It's all the manufacturers' dollars. As I sell the inventory, I pay them. I am able to turn (sell) the inventory quickly enough that as the bills come due, the inventory we have in the building has sold and I'm not necessarily going to the bank to borrow money to pay for inventory," Zane adds.

That scenario doesn't work in all industries. And small businesses often don't understand what amount of inventory is right for their business, adds Zane. How much is the right inventory for your business? That's an individual decision. "You need to be cognizant of how the finances of your particular industry work and how to use those nuances to be most beneficial for you," he says.

Another financial tool to take advantage of is interest-free credit that's offered occasionally. Bank of America, for example, regularly offers us the option to borrow up to $35,000 interest free for six months for a mere $75 fee! These zero-interest deals are great for getting your company through tough periods when cash is tight. Do remember, though, that anything you borrow, with or without interest, has to be paid back. So borrow only what you need and what you can repay. With the *Pacific Coast Business Times*, we usually borrow $20,000 and then pay it back in five payments in order to avoid interest rate charges.

From the Trenches

If a payroll calculation error occurs, don't automatically assume it's your fault. It may not be. Earlier this year our payrolls were running unusually heavy, but I attributed that to what I assumed were one-time California unemployment charges. However, I later learned in an e-mail that the State of California had supplied incorrect information to our payroll company. I subsequently received a credit back to our account. It was small but gratifying because it reaffirmed that my calculations were correct. It also was good to know that my payroll outsourcer was honest, too!

Software Can Work for You

PCs and software have made life both simpler and more complex for you and the Big Boxers. Technology allows you to manage finances at a very low cost. But you must make it work correctly or it can take you further off track. As we've mentioned, consider polishing your skills on financial management computer programs. It will make the inevitable number-crunching much easier and you won't feel as if you're flailing around in a sea of endless figures.

Don't however, try to fit a square peg—your business—into a round hole. There is no one-size-fits-all software solution. Recognize that, and use off-the-shelf programs as a framework for your business's financial reports, but don't expect them to do every report. Don't be shy about creating your own reports using programs such as Excel. It may be the best way to manage cash and make good decisions about when to hire more employees or buy equipment.

Business and industry organizations as well as fellow small-business people—remember, I consulted ad executive Finlon, also in a service industry—can be a great source of report templates, too.

Computer programs aside, get a good bookkeeper, even if it is to work for you only a few hours a month. Whether or not you're a numbers whiz in your own right, that second set of eyes and alternative voice can be invaluable.

■ ■ ■ ■ ■ ■

Salespeople sell and bean counters count. Smart management gets them both on the same team.
—Harvey Mackay

■ ■ ■ ■ ■ ■

Taxes

Small businesses, similar to the Big Boxers down the block, must pay attention to tax issues. Of course, the Big Boxers probably have a few more zeroes to the left of the decimal points in their dollar calculations. It's also easier for them to swallow big tax goofs. So pay attention. No matter how smart you think you are, get professional tax help. Look for a qualified tax expert, preferably a CPA, who understands the numbers, has experience working with small businesses, and knows the corporate tax nuances in your state. You likely can get an initial consultation and set up your business's partnership or corporation for less than $1,000, and maybe even less than $500 if you do your own paperwork, says Iannone.

Whether you choose to develop an ongoing relationship with that or any financial advisor is up to you. But, says Iannone, as a professional financial advisor, "I can help you put together a strategic plan that helps you maximize your potential and your earnings based on whatever widget you invented. And I can help with your annual plan and measuring your performance against that plan."

If your company, no matter how small, has international dealings or subsidiaries, pay attention to how the company is structured, says Iannone. He recounts the story of one client, a U.S. firm with $15 million in revenue that manufactured its products through an overseas subsidiary. If the company hadn't paid attention to very complex tax issues, it could have paid taxes on the overseas manufacturing and sales as well as on its U.S. sales and revenue.

Watch out for those ads on the Internet and the like that tout fast incorporations for a few bucks, too. It's the "you get what you pay for" syndrome. Another big come-on that's simply not true, says Iannone, is "'Incorporate in Nevada and never have liability again.' Plenty of people out there will say, 'We can get you incorporated for $80.' Sure, they can fill out a template for you, but it may have nothing to do with what can be the best structure for you."

Bottom Lines

Be careful with your cash, eBags's Nordmark cautions other entrepreneurs. Don't gamble with the money; take measured risks instead. Test a new product, idea, or approach on a small scale, and if it appears to work, ratchet it up from there. "So many smart people in the dot-bomb spent all the money they had raised in a three-month period, and lost everything," he adds.

Says entrepreneur, small-business woman turned researcher, author, and expert Rogers:

I think the toughest part for many small-business owners is to recognize that all the financial details and more aren't the focus of your business, even though it feels like it. You have to get the licenses from the city; handle the lawyers; work with the accountants to get incorporated; fool with taxes; hire your staff; make sure your payroll is set up, plus you have to set up your store or your product for sale. You have so much to do, and the easy part is to forget the whole reason why you're here. And that reason is the customers you have.

It seems obvious, but the fact is you don't have to have a product to get a business going. What you do have to have is a customer. That's probably the most important, number one thing for a small business to remember. It's your customers who mean you have a business, and all the rest of it is what you do to have customers. You would be amazed at how many companies forget that. Ask a CEO of a very large company where her revenues come from and the answer likely will be, From our great products. Oh, really? Your products pay you money? Well, they don't, but even very smart people forget that.

■ ■ ■ ■ ■ ■ ■ ■

There's no secondary market for customers. You can't just go to a bank, borrow some customers for a while, and pay them back with interest later.

—Don Peppers and Martha Rogers

■ ■ ■ ■ ■ ■ ■ ■ ■

Your Ammunition

Some essentials to remember from this chapter include:

■ As a small-business owner, you don't need to be an economist or a math wizard, but you do need to understand your cost structures and have a detailed and ongoing business plan.

■ Set yourself up to succeed with your detailed plans. That includes a business plan and a budget that you use regularly. You can't account for everything, but at least you will have set goals and a framework to achieve them.

■ In addition to your annual budget, pay attention to your outflow and inflow with the help of weekly reports.

■ Design your business with profitability in mind. In other words, if you can't afford it, don't do it.

■ Insist on financial terms with your clients that enable your business to succeed.

■ Capitalize on trade terms, whether a no-interest credit line offer or financial breaks for early or prompt payment to your vendors, or other financial tools in your industry and from your providers.

CHAPTER
7

RELENTLESS INNOVATION AND VISION

The process of innovation is a primary part of the culture of a successful company.
—Harold S. Edwards, president and CEO, Limoneira Company, Santa Paula, California

Don't believe for a minute that small businesses can't win because their owners shrink from competition with the Big Boxes. Behind every successful small business is a tireless worker and cheerleader who relishes challenge: the small-business owner.

To get ahead and stay ahead, the best companies adopt the Intel model of relentless innovation. That uncompromising goal requires vision—the ability to see past the short term and, instead, look at the big picture of your business, its existing and potential products, your competition, the playing field, and much more both today and in the future. That's a tall order, but it goes with the territory.

189

How important is the long view? Nearly half of all entrepreneurs (47 percent) spend more than 10 hours a week thinking about innovations and new ideas for their business, according to an April 2008 American Express OPEN Small Business Monitor, a semi-annual survey of business owners.[1] More results from that same survey:

- Nearly four in 10 (38 percent) of entrepreneurs "daydream" to spark creativity.
- 34 percent say their best ideas come during down time.
- On average, entrepreneurs spend 13 hours a week thinking creatively about their business.

Vision Equals Innovation

It's easy to fall into a rut and accept the status quo, doing the same thing day in and day out, eking out a bit of profit while working hard, but getting basically nowhere. That's where vision truly can make a difference for your small business.

"Many small businesses repeat bad behaviors that don't work. Consequently, that keeps the business small and lacks vision," says marketing expert Finlon. "Continuous improvement is a very doable and real concept in small business."

Innovation translates to success

The best part about vision is that it doesn't cost anything, yet, as we've shown, it can add big-time to your bottom line. It's all in the approach you—and, in turn, your employees—take. By its very nature, vision leads to innovation, with financial benefit likely to follow.

Remember Imperial Headwear, the small hat manufacturer we talked about earlier? When the company lost a potentially big client for its golf hats because of price point—Imperial wasn't the lowball player on the block—CEO Rick White opened his eyes and his mind to the future. What he saw was more of the same deal-breakers unless he could find a way for the company to clearly differentiate its products. He sent his people back to the drawing board in search of a better, more innovative product for the future. The result was that the company developed hats with clear purposes—from sun protection to moisture wicking, and more.

"In a world that is highly commoditized, to continue to innovate and imagine new opportunities for headwear (or anything else) takes on terrific relevance," says White.

A perfect example is Chris Zane, visionary extraordinaire, and his Zane's Cycles, which he took from only $56,000 a year in sales to $13.5 million and climbing. From a tiny bicycle and hobby shop run by a 16-year-old, Zane's Cycles today is one of the largest bicycle retailers in Connecticut, nationally renowned for offering lifetime guarantees on its products, and one of the largest business-to-business providers of bicycles for company incentive programs in the United States. That's vision. That's long-term thinking, innovation, and execution to a T.

"From Day One, I looked at what all my competitors had and what they didn't have, and how I could change the game on them and make it easier for us to capture market share without having to diminish our profitability," says Zane. "I'm comfortable looking at the long-term solution to a situation, so I looked at the business and said, if I want to be around in 20 or 30 years, I have to build a foundation with customers so they'll keep coming back." He did and they do, as his 25-percent annual growth reflects.

When Jim Wolfe took over a struggling nutrition bar company, instead of accepting the situation as it was, he looked at the big picture and the possibilities beyond the status quo. Maybe the product, he surmised (with the help of market research), wasn't targeting the right audience. The transformation to Balance Bar as a snack and meal-replacement bar was the end result. The transformation led to incredible financial success for the company, its employees, and its shareholders.

Sometimes vision is as simple as a small-business owner having good ideas and being open to change and new ways of doing things. The hugely popular behemoth that is Craigslist.org wasn't always a big winner. In fact, it failed the first time around, says company namesake Newmark, because of his failure as a manager. But Newmark, with the help of others, recognized his shortcomings and brought in Jim Buckmaster as CEO in 2000. "After Jim took over, we just started getting our act together better and better," says Newmark.

eBags's innovation was its business model of drop-shipping products directly from manufacturers as opposed to the more traditional warehouse model as a product storage facility model. That involves complicated and technical behind-the-scenes operations. But the end result is that eBags is able to carry a vast array of product without actually having it lying around in our warehouse, says Nordmark. "We showcase product sitting in our manufacturers' warehouses." The company also was an online pioneer and among the first to feature independent product reviews on its Website. Today that's become standard operating procedure across all kinds of business and industry.

Innovation with purpose

Entrepreneur-turned-mayor-of-Denver Hickenlooper insists he didn't have any great vision, but he did have purpose when he decided to open a brewpub in an historic building in a decaying section of downtown Denver in 1988.

"They called me a fool, a dreamer, a crazy person," says Hickenlooper, at the time an unemployed geologist with entrepreneurial yearnings. "I didn't have any great vision. I just thought it was a beautiful part of the city with all these historic buildings."

Ultimately, Hickenlooper says, he and his partners believed in downtown Denver as a place where people should want to live. They converted the upper floors of their brewpub warehouse into lofts, which were among the first loft living spaces in Denver, a city that today has 25,000 housing units in its downtown area. "We had good core values, and we believed in downtown," Hickenlooper adds.

That moral purpose of looking past the profit was a successful approach that Hickenlooper and his business partners parlayed beyond Denver. "We were in the business of creating jobs and revitalizing downtowns," says Hickenlooper. "We opened restaurants, always in historic buildings and always in downtowns, all over the country. They were all brewpubs, and we ended up with about 17."

The concept and its execution were so successful that the National Trust for Historic Preservation gave Hickenlooper its Award of Honor for his efforts. (When Hickenlooper was elected Denver mayor in 2003, his small-business holdings went into a trust. He later sold those holdings to his former business partner.)

Vision with purpose at travel agency GreatHawaiiVacations.com involves taking a unique approach to the business, especially in the face of adversity, whether economic or natural, such as hurricanes in Hawaii. The company's owners and management put a positive spin even on the most negative situations, and that's a big part of why the company continues to thrive as its competitors struggle in today's tough economic times. "Think of the business as a playground, a sandbox, where maybe the castle you just built fell down," says co-owner Goldberg. "But now look at all the space you have and what new things you can build besides castles. That's the kind of energy and vision that my husband, Joel Goldberg, and our partners, Owen Plant and Eric Kang, have with GreatHawaiiVacations.com."

For Finlon, a big part of the vision she applied to her company involved the courage to continually analyze the company's processes, procedures, and decisions, and jettison or change whatever isn't working. "It takes discipline to discard what you think is fun to do or what you thought worked," says Finlon. "It takes constant analyzing and asking, 'Did that really work? Do I need to change that and take a different route?'"

With J.D. Power and Associates, a strong sense of purpose kept all aspects of the company working toward its vision, says Power. "When my father was building J.D. Power and Associates...the core of keeping things aligned was this incredibly strong sense of mission that we were there to make a difference by using consumer research to make businesses do things better," says Power. "It's wasn't *Consumer Reports* (the magazine) or Ralph Nader (legendary consumer advocate). It was working with businesses to help them improve."

When Harold Edwards, with his broad-reaching vision, took the helm of Limoneira Company in Ventura County, California, five years ago, the 115-year-old agricultural giant was struggling. Despite what Edwards refers to as the company's "amazing assets" in terms of capital, land, water, and brand equity, the company had stopped performing and instead was focused on preserving its assets in their current state. "They had stopped innovating, stopped playing offense, and just played defense," he says. "People were hanging their heads and saying the party is over."

But Edwards wasn't willing to accept that assessment. The then-agriculture-only company had been founded on principles that called for stewardship of resources, the environment, land, and water. Profit was the by-product, says Edwards. So he put a 21st century spin on that vision and expanded the company from strictly farming to agribusiness, community development, and also stewardship (read that taking a leadership role in the community). He capitalized on the company's vast housing (at the time well-below-market rents) and real estate holdings, leveraged relationships with marketers, and forged a partnership with the local community (Santa Paula, California) to develop a master, sustainable growth plan. The plan was sustainable, Edwards says, because it had something in it for everyone.

Today Limoneira is a world leader in agriculture production: It's the largest lemon producer in North America, the largest avocado producer in the United States, and a big producer in oranges, specialty citrus, pistachios, and more. It's also a leader in sustainability farming operations, land development, and community development. It has not always been easy, either. The company suffered a multiyear loss in avocados when a big freeze hit California and, with its big real estate holdings, has some exposure to California's sagging real estate market. But the vision perseveres. "The process of innovation is a primary part of the culture of a successful company," adds Edwards.

Learning and Growing Your Business

The good news is that you can learn to develop vision. It's quite simple: Open your eyes to reality, and then think long instead of short. Look beyond the obvious and recognize how your business can survive and thrive in the future instead of only until tomorrow.

Change can energize a business

MackayMitchell Envelope was a small business struggling to survive when owner Harvey Mackay had a chance encounter that changed his company forever. He learned that a different vision of his company's trash—the waste left from the envelope-manufacturing process—could pay big dividends. Mackay says:

When I first started out in the envelope business, I just couldn't figure out how to make a buck. There was too much competition, the margins were—you guessed it—paper-thin, and it seemed as if I was constantly under pressure to go into debt to buy newer, faster equipment. I went to my first trade show hoping to get a clue, and wound up at the lounge of the Fairmont Hotel in San Francisco at 2 a.m. with a man whose last name is lost forever to me but whose first name I'll never forget. His first name was actually Goldberg, a good ol' boy from the

Deep South, whose daddy had given him his 'Christian' name in honor of a rabbi he admired.

"'How the heck do you make a buck in this business?' I asked him.

"'D'pends on how much you get fo' the scrap,' the wise man said.

"'The what?' I asked.

"'The scrap; the scrap, the wastage! Your leftover paper. How much a ton are you gettin' up there where you live? You got a good contract, you make out good; bad contract, you make out good, too, just not quite as good.'

"I, of course, had been paying some guys to haul the scrap away. Didn't everyone? Apparently not. My competitors were getting $250 a ton from the same guys. Scrap is now a major profit center at MackayMitchell Envelope, which is why we can practically *give* those envelopes away," says Mackay.

Giant Weyerhaeuser Company, the world's largest forest-products company, learned a similar lesson in waste, says Mackay. The company didn't know what to do with the tremendous volume of sawdust it generated. But it knew there had to be a better use for it than as trash, and it finally developed a new technology to compress that waste into solid board.

"Waste is an inescapable fact of life in countless industries," adds Mackay. "But waste stops being waste when you package it for someone who wants it. Most businesses aren't like Steuben or Waterford where the craftsman can just melt the glass down on the spot when a piece is flawed. In all kinds of industries, what you do with the waste or the rejects can spell the difference between breaking through and breaking down.

"Think out of the box; think visionary in your own small business. Do you have a waste or leftover product or service that fits the 'one person's trash is another's treasure' scenario? If so, think about how to package it, market it, and boost your bottom line in the process," advises Mackay.

■ ■ ■ ■ ■ ■

Always tailor your research and product development
investment toward real-world action. Information
does not become power until it is used.

—Harvey Mackay

■ ■ ■ ■ ■ ■ ■

Looking beyond the existing product to create something new and different and out of the box was how we came up with the Spirit of Small Business Awards we talked about in Chapter 4. The awards also helped energize the bottom line, our staff, and the community.

Not only do the awards recognize local businesses and entrepreneurs, but they also are a great marketing/branding platform for our publication and further link us to our customers, advertisers, and the community. It's a perfect marriage for all parties. And it happened because we had eyes open to innovation and change.

From the Trenches

Dare to dream big and set your goals high! That's what we did at the *Pacific Coast Business Times,* and we not only achieved our goals, but surpassed them.

From the beginning, I decided not only to start a successful business journal, but to tailor it to meet the specifications of the City Business Journals Network. The network, which is owned by the parent company of my former employer, the *Denver Business Journal,* provides national advertising to local business journals and takes a pretty sizable commission to do so. But it also recognizes exclusive territories, which gives any network member a big leg up on potential competitors. By the end of 2002, we felt we had met the requirements—a quality editorial product, a small but credible list of paid subscribers, and financial results that were break-even on an operating basis—and had done so for some time. Through the years, I also had kept in touch with network president George Conley.

In 2003, our admission to the network was a significant watershed for our company. We immediately received orders for a half-dozen full-page, four-color ads from Xerox. These were huge, and our network business soon became a significant source of advertising revenue. If we hadn't had the vision to shoot high in the beginning, our company might not have had its tremendous and ongoing success, or at least not as quickly.

Unlike our Big Box neighbors, we small businesses have the advantage of being able to innovate and change quickly and at will—our nimble, niche advantage. Remember, though, to thoroughly and honestly evaluate your business's individual situation—thinking through the positives and negatives of any change—before making your move. After all, not ALL change is good. Change can alienate your core customers as easily as it can grow your customer base. We all probably can think of at least one small business that made a substantial change, drove off its customers, and ended up a failure. Tread carefully, but do move, because if you don't, the competition will pass you by.

Time to spare

As owner of your business, you may be thinking, "Yeah, right. This all sounds good, but I'm already overworked. Where am I going to find the time to daydream about my business's future?"

That's where cycle maven Zane's 2,000 hours a year focusing on learning all aspects of your business comes in very handy. "Too many business owners get tied up in busywork because they are afraid to relinquish control; they can't delegate, and they don't have teams built up underneath them to handle operations. So they wind up running around doing all the things they should be paying people to do so they can become the expert in their industry," adds Zane.

Zane's management team includes four individuals who handle the day-to-day finance, operations, national sales, and retail of his company with its 50 employees, and these four report to him directly. "They know I can jump in and do whatever it is they do because I have spent the time building the business and understand each of their operations," says Zane. "But at the end of the day, my responsibility is to find growth opportunities (read that "vision and innovation"), and their responsibility is to run the company."

Building Your Strategic Team

Whether your business has a handful of employees or 500, you, too, need a strategic team. Sure, you might start your entrepreneurial adventure with a staff of one—yourself—but even then you have a strategic team—those people you count on for advice, as a sounding board, for answers to legal questions, and more. They're not only there to plug the holes, but to fix them, too. If you've chosen your team correctly, they'll anticipate many of those holes before they appear. One of the toughest jobs faced by most small-business owners is to let go and delegate processes, procedures, and leadership to others.

The members of your team and their various areas of expertise and skills depend on your own expertise, your business, your business's needs, and more. As we've mentioned, the most important thing is to recognize your shortcomings and realize that, just as you can't do it without your employees, you can't go it alone without advisors, either.

From the Trenches

My advisor team: Through the years, many people have helped our company and me personally get a handle on the situation and move the company forward. Typically, these were not highly compensated people, but they were professionals who, for one reason or another, came to realize how important our mutual alignment of interests really was. Through time their advice became critically important to the success of the company.

My team of advisors includes:

- **John Huggins:** Our vice chairman has been there from the beginning. He is patient, calm, analytical, and a helpful listener. He also knows California and the quirks of its labor laws, having been the CFO of a Newport Beach, California–based software company in the 1990s. But, most of all, he's 100 percent in my corner—honest in his criticism but always willing to encourage. All are important attributes for an advisor.

- **Phil Drescher:** Our local counsel, he knows how to size up a tactical situation and get to the problem. He's Mr. Common Sense, very eager to find solutions that are quick, easy, and cheap, and then get out of the way. He has a well-deserved reputation for being a trusted business advisor as much as a lawyer.

- **Ana Mercer:** Our Wells Fargo commercial banker. She died after a long bout with breast cancer this past summer in 2008. But before that, even though she was supposed to be banking companies much larger than ours, she took a personal interest in our business and was there countless times for us. She coached, cajoled, listened, and helped our company get to breakeven or better. She also taught me the importance of operating profits—of building a company that would operate at better than breakeven over an extended period so we could build a cash cushion for the future and not have to rely on expensive credit lines to fund operations. Every small business can benefit from an Ana Mercer.

■ **David Uhler and Grace Stalica:** Our CPAs at Bartlett Pringle & Wolf both have been extremely helpful through the years in sorting out my personal financial situation from that of the company and helping both stand alone. They've helped me learn that tax considerations are only part of the picture—that an entrepreneur needs a strong personal balance sheet to be an effective leader and to focus on building the business. Surprisingly, as my own cash position strengthened, so did the company's, and my compensation actually went up.

■ **Kerry McCoy:** Our HR consultant at HR Express in Santa Barbara, she knows California labor law inside and out, and is keenly aware of the problems of finding and keeping employees in an expensive locale like coastal California. She's also taught me how to motivate marginal employees into becoming strong performers and how to deal with people whose personal lives make it difficult for them to commit to their jobs. She's built a strong set of employment policies for us and helped us gain a reputation as a fair and honorable employer.

■ ■ ■ ■ ■ ■ ■ ■
Advice or Not

The NFIB Research Foundation surveyed small employers—those with one to 250 employees—about their use of advisors.[2] *Among the findings:*

- *66 percent of small-business owners have one person they are likely to consult before making a critical business decision; in order of frequency, that person is a spouse, a partner/co-owner, a professional advisor/counselor, an employee, and a son.*

- *34 percent of small-business owners have no one person they turn to prior to making a critical business decision; 55 percent of those owners handle the decision solo, and the rest either change the advisor with the situation/decision or routinely consult with several people.*

- *In the past 12 months, 84 percent of small employers sought advice from one or more counselors (people not in the firm and not the firm's customers).*

- *59 percent sought advice from an accountant; the next most commonly solicited advisors were family members (44 percent), lawyers (39 percent), other business owners (34 percent), suppliers (31 percent), and insurance agents and brokers (30 percent).*

- *The advice solicited from counselors was commonly taken. However, a relationship appeared between the likelihood of taking the advice and paying for the advice. The chances of taking advice rose when small-business owners paid for it.*

- *Small-business men and women often did not pay for the advice that they received or they paid for it indirectly through purchase of other goods and services. However, payment (or the lack thereof) was tied to the type of advisor.*

- *57 percent percent of small employers say that they received helpful, unsolicited suggestions from an advisor or other non-customer outside the firm in the last year.*

- *Accounting, bookkeeping, and taxes were the subjects on which advice was most frequently sought.*

■ *Advice was also frequently sought on legal questions (56 percent), computers, software, Websites and telecommunications (53 percent), and industry-specific technical matters (48 percent).*

Source: NFIB Research Foundation.

■ ■ ■ ■ ■ ■ ■

The coach option

Whether you choose to have a personal coach or even a confidant or advisor as part of your strategic team is a personal choice, says well-known personal coach McKee. "But you can't monitor yourself."

McKee is right with that observation. We all need someone to whom we can at least bounce ideas off and who looks out for our interests if we truly hope to excel long term. Whoever that person is and whatever title he has or hat she wears, he or she should be someone you're comfortable with. That person could be an advisor with SCORE, a professional coach, a confidant, spouse, significant other, or any myriad other people. It's unlikely, though, that a single "coach" will be able to provide all the advice or direction you as a small-business owner might need. After all, how many individuals can do it all—from navigating HR issues to cash management, inventory management, sales, marketing, business in general, and more? The key, as we've said before, is to recognize your weaknesses and realize that a strategic *team* works to the advantage of you and your business.

"Some of my clients refer to me as their 'business partner,'" says McKee. "That's in quotes, but basically they are saying, 'I have somebody who cares about my business, who doesn't have any ulterior motives, and who I can bounce ideas off.' They also can talk about skills they don't have."

Recognize your limitations, too, says McKee. "Often by the time I see small-business people, they're burned out. When they start out and they're very enthusiastic and they think they love it so much that they're working night and day and weekends, and then they lose their perspective entirely. That's when you really need to have a business partner who has no vested interest except to make you more successful."

Craigslist's Newmark laments that, the first time around with his Website, he didn't have an advisor or coach. "I would have done a better job if I had had a good one!"

Cathey Finlon had owned her advertising agency for about eight years when she hit a wall. A significant and favorite client was at risk of no longer doing business with the company and, at the same time, Finlon says,

> The firm had grown, everyone was working, but we weren't getting anywhere. I felt the fault was either with the management I'd surrounded myself with or me. So I reached out to find a consultant to advise me and help me, because I was stuck.
>
> I thought I wanted a planning consultant to help with management, and I ended up with an entrepreneur who coached me into understanding that if I wanted to change the way the organization worked, I had to change. What I realized was I had to create space for a better management to operate. I had to step back, let go, and be a different kind of controlling and learn to be more encouraging.

The end result was that she restructured her management and hired a president, and the firm blossomed. The agency eventually lost that favorite client, but it no longer mattered.

Coach or mentor

A mentor differs from a coach, says McKee, in that a mentor usually is someone proficient in a given field or organization. A coach is not necessarily a specialist in a specific field. He or she is trained to ask questions that you may not have considered, to give feedback about what you're doing, and to help you understand new ways of doing business that you haven't tried or tested before. "A coach can be more of a safe haven than a mentor," McKee adds.

Affordability

A coach needn't cost a ton of money, either. You can find a good coach for as little as $150 an hour and use him or her for a couple of hours a month, perhaps, as a wakeup call, says McKee.

Finding the right coach

Sources of possible coaches include small-business associations, local and national industry organizations, the International Coach Federation (*www.coachfederation.org*), and the Worldwide Association of Business Coaches (*www.wabccoaches.com*). McKee also suggests buying groups, associations that negotiate discount prices on goods and services based on the power of volume buying. He is associated with The Buying Group (*www.thebuyinggroup.com*). SCORE, an acronym for Senior Corps of Retired Executives, closely associated with the SBA is another great source that can provide free and confidential coaching by experts.

As with any consultant or contractor, thoroughly check a coach's qualifications, get references, and follow through and check them. Rapport with a prospective coach is especially important. If the two of you don't click, cross that coach off your list and move on to the next potential candidate.

■ ■ ■ ■ ■ ■ ■ ■ ■

Tips to Finding the Right Coach

John M. McKee, business and career success coach and author of *Career Wisdom: 101 Proven Strategies to Ensure Workplace Success* (Wheatmark, 2007) and *21 Ways Women in Management Shoot Themselves in the Foot* (Wheatmark, 2006), offers a few suggestions to help you find the right coach:

- ■ Does the potential coach have experience in your field or dealing with similar types of businesses or situations?
- ■ Ask for testimonials from other clients or whether you can contact those clients.

■ Is the individual certified as a coach (the primary certification comes from the International Coach Federation)? It's not uncommon for people—unemployed or otherwise—to hang up a shingle and claim they're a "coach" or "consultant" whether they're qualified or not.

■ Will the individual or organization guarantee results or provide a money-back promise? The best coaches are confidant enough in their work to provide this assurance up front. If a potential coach won't, you should wonder why not.

Your investors as advisors

A company investor can be a great advisor, too, especially if your small business counts on funding from angel investors with vested interest in your success. These people often become an entrepreneur's lead coach, not for the revenue but for the challenge and satisfaction of educating and mentoring an entrepreneur. Of course, added financial success on the part of the company is incentive, too.

John Huggins was one of our angel investors, and with his broad business and entrepreneurial expertise, he became my perfect guide to business. As an investor in our company, he also had a vested interest in seeing our venture succeed.

Your Long-Term Role

What exactly is your long-term role in your small business? That depends on many factors, and not just whether the business succeeds beyond your wildest dreams.

As a small-business owner, you must address the what-ifs. Otherwise, you could wake up one day and find yourself in a future with no idea where to go or what to do.

Those what-ifs include:

- What if the business is successful?
- What if the business isn't successful?
- What if you decide to leave the business to pursue other interests?
- What if you decide to retire?
- What if you die suddenly or suffer major health problems?
- What if you're forced to sell the business for one reason or another?

An entrepreneur needs to consider these questions when putting together a business plan. You don't have to know the answers to all these questions before you open your doors, but you should at least consider them and have answers for some. After all, your small business is, in many ways, like a child. You wouldn't fail to plan for your child's care should something happen to you.

Retire or regroup?

Entrepreneurs are optimistic by nature and generally require ongoing challenges to be truly satisfied. The same routine day in and day out, no matter how stimulating, can get old—as can the struggle to create and sustain your business's success.

Just ask Finlon. This year, at age 62 and after 24 years with a successful advertising business, she again paid attention to the economy, recognized her firm was about to lose a major client, and decided to downsize to a marketing consulting firm. "I'm ready for a new challenge," Finlon says.

Craigslist's Newmark, as mentioned earlier, chose to step back, regroup his company, and concentrate on that aspect of the business he did best: customer service. Today his role is to represent his company and serve as a customer service representative. His title is Founder and Customer Service Representative.

The Internet and subsequent technology boom has meant that many entrepreneurial start ups consider initial public offerings or sale a primary goal, too. For John Huggins and his founding partners, for example, selling their software start-up company represented the achievement of their goal. It also meant sizable financial reward because their company's buyer, AOL, was young at the time and could afford to pay only in stock. Lucky for Huggins and his partners!

Other entrepreneurs opt to grow their businesses on a much smaller level and then sell or even close and take on an entirely new challenge. Remember New York–based SCORE counselor Lehman who offered his advice earlier? He was co-owner of a small chain of women's apparel stores in Ohio and Pennsylvania for five years before internal differences between the partners forced the chain to close. But that didn't stop Lehman. He took on another challenge, joining SCORE as its chief marketer in New York and serving as a SCORE counselor. He now helps other small businesses, using the knowledge he gained during his years in the retail business. For an entrepreneur, there's always a next step.

Full-time visionary?

Vision is an essential part of life for small-business owners. For those who have their operations and staff running smoothly—think successful entrepreneurs—it's a full- or nearly full-time job. The hours spent on innovation ultimately net big results, and if you don't do it, who will?

"I can't hire a futurist," says Holstein. "As an owner, you can either do it yourself or not." Last year alone, his vision translated to $10.2 million in sales, up 37 percent and still growing. Zane's vision translated into an increase in sales of more than 24,000 percent!

Innovation and change are the keys to success, to your business staying fresh. And, frankly, change is more fun than working in a stagnant environment, says David Peterson, owner of six

McDonald's franchises in Southern California. "You constantly have to keep reinventing yourself."

Peterson is the son of and was a partner with his visionary father, Herb Peterson, inventor of the venerable Egg McMuffin. "My dad came up with the Egg McMuffin when I was in junior high," recalls Peterson. "We weren't open for breakfast at the time, and my dad felt we should be. He loved Eggs Benedict and found a way to create a handheld Eggs Benedict. It was a small idea that revolutionized McDonald's and the breakfast industry around the world."

The older Peterson died in spring 2008. But his vision and innovation remain legendary. In fact, says David, his father, who had a background in advertising, played a role in the creation of the image of Ronald McDonald as a symbol for McDonald's.

"Every innovation doesn't always work," adds Peterson, who carries on the tradition of vision and innovation as well as the business success of his father. "But that doesn't mean you should stop innovating. Of the innovations that I try in our restaurants, maybe one out of 10 works, but that one is a home run."

Those innovations go beyond products, he says. They can be people practices, customer service, the way you treat your employees, discipline practices, and much more.

"I guided innovation by staying out of the way and supporting innovative people," says Kinko's founder Orfalea. "As the founder and senior partner, I could have dictated anything, but once you start doing that, you demoralize your workforce and end up having to dictate everything. You need people to make good decisions for themselves. You might be able to require white paint and blue counters, but can you dictate a passion for customer service? Your company's level of innovation will be determined, to a great extent, by the level of personal trust between you and your coworkers."

Exit Strategies

Whether you like it or not, this is another case of short-term planning for the long term. An exit strategy generally is part of your business plan, too.

For some entrepreneurs and their companies, eBusiness expert Daniel Meyerov, among them the exit strategy and the business plan go hand in hand. "We started the companies with the idea of selling them," says Meyerov, successful entrepreneur and 12-year veteran Website designer. He's a co-founder with Mark Friedman of OnlyBusiness.com, a one-stop affordable shop for small business owners looking to establish and maintain a solid Web presence, and Polaris Blue (*www.polarisblue.com*), a design firm that serves CBS Television's reality programming needs and small-business Web strategies.

Meyerov isn't alone in his goal of selling. Venture capitalists and entrepreneurs by the thousands invest millions every year with the hope of building highly successful companies to take public through an IPO, or to sell. For others, such as Finlon, the entrepreneurial dream calls for a long-term commitment to their company.

eBags's Nordmark didn't start his business to sell it. But, he adds, "We've been approached by a lot of companies, and the reality of business is that once you've taken on investors, you do owe them an ability to get out."

"I'm an almost-textbook entrepreneur," adds Zane. "If I do something for a while, I get bored. Once I've figured it out, I have no interest in doing it again. If I were still standing around the store selling bicycles one at a time and having conversations, I could do it. But I wouldn't be happy, I wouldn't be challenged, and I'd be less than passionate about it. Over time I've realized that in order to be successful, I have to find new things. So I'm responsible for the growth of our company, because growth is all about new things."

Knowing when to split

Recognizing when to call it quits and move on is a tough call for which there's no right answer. Plenty of entrepreneurs struggle every day but keep at it, while others turn and walk away. Beyond the dollars and cents, your gut feelings play a big part in that decision.

"Every small-business owner or entrepreneur is going to have those days when everything goes wrong, when it seems impossibly difficult, and you feel like you're working for $2 an hour," says angel investor Huggins. "There has to be some ingredient, a native optimism, a determination to succeed. There has to be something within you that makes you get up and keep going the next morning. If you as an entrepreneur don't have that, you probably aren't going to succeed."

But there is no litmus test for that indefinable ingredient, Huggins adds. "In my experience as an investor, you don't know if someone has it until you see them go through really difficult periods and get up every day and hurl themselves against the wall."

Huggins recounts the story of two young entrepreneurs involved in a startups he had helped to fund. "Both worked tirelessly to make their businesses work. It wasn't until they had exhausted all the possibilities that each gave up. In both cases, I felt the obligation to let them off the hook (for any repayment of investment) because they had worked so hard to make their business succeed."

For SCORE counselor Lehman, what counts is if you can get up in the morning and say, "I want to go to work," and you're happy doing what you're doing and feel fulfilled, no matter your age.

Succession planning

If your small business is family owned, it's important to make contingency plans for a smooth transition should you decide to leave the business or even die. If your exit strategy calls for selling the business—to an insider or someone else—or passing it on to your heirs, you had better make sure it's spelled out to the last detail up front and in writing. That takes legal advice from qualified individuals who have experience dealing with similar transactions. After all, you want to make sure your wishes are carried out. No matter how simple you think a transaction might be, it isn't and won't be.

Your Ammunition

Some essentials to remember from this chapter include:

- Don't just sit back and accept the status quo. Look ahead, innovate, and grow for the better.

- That ability to innovate and change is one of the biggest assets a small business has.

- The right kind of change can energize your business. Be open to new ideas, products, services, and approaches whether your own, from your employees, from your competitor's, or from somewhere or someone else.

- Set yourself up to succeed with the right group of strategic advisors who complement your strengths and weaknesses. And be painfully honest in the assessment of your abilities.

- Consider the possibility of a coach if you feel you may be particularly weak in a skill level.

- Devote a specific amount of time regularly to think about new innovations for your company.

- Think about an exit plan from your business, too. You don't need to dwell on it; just recognize its importance, and address it.

CHAPTER
8

YOUR BATTLE PLAN: PUTTING IT ALL TOGETHER

To succeed long term, you must learn how to balance the demands of all the competing interests in your company, from customers and the community to employees, providers, suppliers, your family, and even yourself.
—Henry Dubroff

Now that you know the players, their positions, and your business's potential in the battle for long-term success, it's time to put it all together to create a plan of attack. As we've talked about throughout this book, your job as owner/operator of your small business isn't to wield an order book. It's to build up the business and keep it running smoothly. You are the primary cheerleader, revenue monitor, keeper of the brand, creator of the business's culture, and visionary. You're also chief of quality control.

Remember, too, that your battle plans will have to account for the positives along with the negatives that at times likely will include cash shortfalls, glitches in plans, equipment malfunctions, missed directions, lost cues, and plenty more of the unexpected. The Big Box competition may be able to afford such missteps, but you and your small business can't afford them now or down the road.

From the Trenches

As I make decisions for the company, much of what I think about is how to balance all the competing interests.

- Employees want decent pay, good benefits, and to work with a fun and cooperative team.
- Customers want service and great prices.
- Community organizations want me to speak or provide media sponsorship advertising that could help build our brand, but also could be a waste of time and space.
- The news team, which still operates generally under my direction, wants mentoring, sources, story ideas, and an occasional stimulating conversation about public policy or First Amendment rights. They also want to plot their next career move.

So, much of what I do is try to keep the company's reputation for breaking news and covering the waterfront intact while meeting all the other obligations. I don't mind making a spur-of-the-moment news decision. But, the business of running the business is a different story. I clear the clutter of day-to-day junk, and then think my decisions all the way through to the company's balance sheet.

As we hope you've learned in this book, long-term success isn't easy, isn't quick, and can't be achieved alone. But it can be extremely rewarding personally, professionally, and financially. Success isn't a one-shot deal, either. You don't simply get your business on track, then sit back and relax long term. Small-business ownership demands that you delegate, yet still pay ongoing attention to your operations. Let's look more closely at how all that melds with the five essentials for long-term success—employee empowerment, small business finances, branding, customers and sales, and vision—and helps ensure your victory in the battle for success.

Embrace Your Customers and Your Business

No matter your business, your goal should be to differentiate yourself and your company, to add value to your goods or services so that you stand out above and beyond your competition. Your customers demand no less. If you don't deliver, they'll go elsewhere.

The "happy" factor

As Grandparents.com's Shereshewsky talked about in Chapter 4, you as owner/operator must figure out how to augment the expected and deliver your generic product or service with enhancements that surprise and delight the customer. It may sound far-fetched, but consider yourself as a customer or client. You likely can get the same product or service from plenty of businesses. Why do you choose a particular one? It's those enhancements that surprise and delight, whether the enhancement is in the service, the product, the innovation, the excellence, or, better still, all of the above. Approach your own business from the customer's viewpoint.

It's all about making your customers happy, says entrepreneur-turned-Denver's-mayor Hickenlooper. "Even while I was running the restaurants, the whole trick was to make sure the managers had the authority to make our customers happy. In the restaurant business, like in many small businesses, your real job is to create joy. So, if a customer has a problem or an unhappy experience, you have to make sure your managers are empowered to make it right, whatever it takes," says Hickenlooper.

Whether you're running a city or a restaurant, many of the basic tenets are the same, he adds. "You never have enough money; you have a diverse group of people you have to make into a team, and the public is always upset about something. You learn that there's no profit margin in having enemies and you do everything you can to make sure every customer, even if they're not perfectly happy, feels they've been heard."

Ask yourself the following questions about your own business:

- Are your employees or managers empowered? Do they have the authority to make decisions to solve problems and satisfy customers and clients?

- Does your business offer a value-added product or service?

- Does your business, product, or service differentiate itself so it stands out ahead of your competition?

For long-term business success, you should have answered yes to all of the above. If not, honestly figure out why not, and then determine what you can do to change any no to a yes. Your long-term success depends on it.

Heed the clues/take the cues

Listen to your company. Pay attention to what's happening internally and externally, and then learn to anticipate and plan for the unexpected that inevitably comes with the turf. If your small business suddenly lurches into fast-growth mode, you'll likely experience growing pains that can range from a critical equipment breakdown to an overwhelmed employee who messes up big time or simply ups and quits. At the other end of the spectrum, if business is painfully slow, you'll likely run into supplier or cash issues, not to mention disgruntled employees. Expect problems, anticipate them, and either have processes in place to handle the situations or be ready to solve the problems on the spot.

A number of years ago advertising executive Finlon picked up on the clues that her firm was about to lose a major client. She took the cue that things weren't working, and looked to a coach to get her company back on track. Just this past year, she again looked at the economy, saw that her firm was about to lose a major client, and came to the conclusion that perhaps she didn't want to deal with rebuilding the firm yet again, so she decided to retire and move on.

When we went into the Southern California marketplace (Santa Barbara to be specific) to launch the *Pacific Coast Business Times*, we originally hadn't planned to buy any existing publication. But after further research—picking up on clues—we decided that it would be better for us to buy our existing competition, the *Business Digest*, instead of starting from scratch. (As I mentioned earlier, I was worried a big competitor had gotten wind of our plans and would buy the *Digest* to compete head on with us.) Six weeks after that acquisition, we had all the infrastructure we needed to launch a bare-bones weekly business journal, including a 1,500-person mailing list, basic advertising agreements, a salesperson, a group of freelancers and columnists, a 30-day credit relationship with a printer and a mail house, and an instant reputation for being the big dog in the market.

From the Trenches

Missed clues and overlooked cues cost us financially early on. In trying to promote the *Pacific Coast Business Times* before it actually launched, we bought a direct mail list and did a direct mailing to the tune of $30,000. It didn't work. Why not? I'm still not absolutely sure, although I think it related to the conservative nature of our advertisers, many of whom waited a year and even two years or longer to see if we'd still be in business before spending their advertising dollars with us. In retrospect, I should have met more with potential advertisers and more thoroughly researched their spending habits. I might have picked up on the clues that they weren't likely to spend money with us right away, and I could have saved the $30,000 for the tough times that followed.

Mackay's mistakes to avoid

Longtime success Harvey Mackay has assembled his list of the biggest mistakes small businesses make:

- Behaving like a *large* business owner tops the list.

- Beware spontaneous decisions you will live with a lifetime. Had a great October? Let's buy everyone a Thanksgiving turkey! You may be handing out 10 this year, but the number could rise to 152 next November.

- Operating without a meaningful plan. Dreams are only dreams unless you have a plan. A goal is a dream with a deadline.

- Ignoring the Law of Large Numbers. If you can't be Number One, the best position you can shoot for is Number Two. It doesn't matter if it's politics or business, Number Two is the strongest position because, when Number One has trouble or messes up in some way, Two is there to take over. Some motivated people think of second place as losing, but it isn't. Apply the Law of Large Numbers to your sales/client prospect list. Position yourself as Number Two to every prospect on your list, and keep adding to that list. I can promise you that if your list is long enough, there will be Number Ones who retire, die, are terminated, or lose their territories for a hundred reasons, and succumb to the Law of Large Numbers. What I can't tell you is which one. If you are standing second in line, in enough lines, sooner or later you're going to move up to number one.

Plans and more planning

Successful entrepreneurs never tire of envisioning their plans for their business, their direction, their goals.

The Issue of Quality Control

Whatever your small business and whatever your plans for it, maintaining the quality of your product or service is an absolute must. With your competition poised to strike at any weakness, you simply can't afford to come up short on quality, period. No matter your big ideas, awesome plans, or level of funding, without consistent quality control you're doomed. That's a guarantee, and you won't find many of those in business today.

What is it?

In many ways, quality control is the culmination of all five major aspects of your business working in sync, with a little added insurance. It's the *perfect* attack team with the full competitive battlefield in mind—your company's finances on solid ground, your marketing/branding on target, your employees well trained and empowered to win, and your long-range vision engaged with innovation in mind. In other words, everyone is on their toes and attuned to making the business work.

That all sounds great, but unfortunately it's not quite enough to ensure your long-term success. Again, you need that bit of extra insurance. You must have fail-safe quality-control measures in place.

Spell it out

Expectations regarding quality need to be in writing and shared with all your employees. Be specific, and have methods in place to measure whether quality control is being met. For example, the quality of your product/service should be an item addressed in regular employee performance reviews. If quality is not up to standards, employees need to know it. They also need to know exactly how they can improve. And, as with other aspects of your small business, don't forget to recognize and reward those employees whose work consistently meets and exceeds your quality standards.

Sometimes small businesses especially fail to recognize the importance of spelling out in detail what's expected of an employee. We've already discussed the importance of taking HR seriously, whether in-house or outsourced.

Pay attention to detail

If yours is a business that involves service, have you called your help desk, service desk, and/or front desk lately? If you haven't, you should as the business's owner, and do it regularly. If you don't like what you hear or see, do something constructive about it. That doesn't mean fire everyone or scream and yell at them either. At one time or another, most of us have watched or had to deal with the distasteful boss who lost his or her temper. And we've seen that it solves nothing. Instead, take the time to analyze the problems, and with your strategic staff, develop ways to fix them. As should be standard operating proceedure with quality issues, be sure to put down in writing what you expect of your employees in terms of service, help, and more.

■ ■ ■ ■ ■ ■

Have you called your help desk lately? You should.

■ ■ ■ ■ ■ ■

Remember when we talked about how Gevalia launched its U.S. mail order operations in Chapter 4? Shereshewsky, one of the masterminds of the effort, talked about the branding representatives standing by 24/7 at the call centers to make sure customers' experiences were positive. That was in the early 1980s. Gevalia is still around and brewing strong numbers.

Call your competition's help desk regularly, too. It pays to know what they're doing and how they handle their customers. That way you can enhance the experience for your own customers. That's one way GreatHawaiiVacations.com, makes sure it's providing its clients the best possible service.

Know your business, your product/ service, your customers

How do you know if you're providing an enhanced product (goods or services) for your clients? First, as cycle maven Zane suggested, know everything possible about your business. Is it clicking on every possible cylinder? If so, and that's a big *"if,"* it usually should show in your bottom line. It also should be reflected in a customer base that includes lots of repeat customers.

Market research

If your bottom line and customer base don't indicate enough product enhancement to satisfy your clients, you need to do market research to find out why not and where you fall short. That doesn't necessarily mean spending a bundle of cash, but you do need to understand your business well enough to spend your money on the right research. When Jim Wolfe first joined a struggling nutrition bar company, the company knew something was amiss and already had spent plenty of dollars on research. But, says Wolfe, its management didn't know the food business, and they didn't know exactly what to research. As a result, the company squandered a lot of money. Because he had a background in food marketing and the market research associated with it, Wolfe knew how to target the research effectively and turn around the company, which became Balance Bar.

Market research doesn't have to be complicated. It can be as simple as talking to potential and existing customers. Ask them what they like and don't like about your products or service, your company, and more. When Wolfe wanted to find out whether people liked the nutrition bar, a couple of his employees would set up a table outside a natural foods store on a Saturday and taste-test the product. The company also sent out questionnaires to its existing customer base and provided incentives in the form of free product for their responses. That was in 1995, before the Internet became the driving force it is today. It's much easier to do market research with the Web as a tool, adds Wolfe.

Your experience

If you're planning a start up, stop and ask yourself whether you have experience and knowledge in the field before you spend your time and money. If you don't, look for another business. If yours is an existing small business that's struggling, is it perhaps because you lack expertise and truly don't know or understand the particular business or industry you're in? If so, face the fact and make changes. Learn about your industry through trade organizations, self-study, or even academic experiences. In the meantime, hire someone who does understand the industry and its nuances. That's what the predecessor to Balance Bar did when it hired Wolfe. "They had bright people," says Wolfe. "They just didn't know what to do in the food business."

Craiglist's Newmark also needed an expert manager. It's hardly surprising that he found his CEO, Jim Buckmaster, on—where else?—Craigslist.org. Buckmaster joined the team, and the rest is Craigslist history.

SCORE counselor Lehman recounts the tale of a client with big plans for starting a restaurant. "I asked him what kind of experience he had, and his response was, 'My mother is a good cook.' I sent him out to get more experience!"

The schmooze factor

Talk to your customers and potential customers as well as your employees periodically about product or service quality, too. What do they like and dislike? What works and what doesn't? Ask for suggestions and listen to them. Most importantly, as advertising entrepreneur Finlon has suggested, be willing to fix what doesn't work.

It's the schmooze factor applied to quality control. Domino's franchisee Hishmeh meets with every one of his employees and is out in the community with his charitable marketing, too. "People love to do business with people they know, they like, and they trust," Hishmeh adds.

Think details and long term. If yours is a product, does the packaging promote a satisfactory customer experience? The packaging could be as fancy as Gevalia coffee's, or as simple as the plastic bag used for many of CableOrganizer.com's products. In fact, in some cases the emphasis better be on simplicity. How many times have you as a consumer ended up fuming at a plastic bag that refuses to open? Overcomplicated packaging can become an irritant to your customers, and potentially cause them to venture elsewhere for the product. Packaging-related cost considerations are another factor to keep in mind, says Holstein. Not only does over-packaging drive up prices and harm the environment, it can actually detract from the inherent value of the product itself, he adds. Pay attention to those details.

Think creatively about your own situation and how to monitor your company's quality. Whether your business is goods or services, beyond calling your own service desk or office phone, get feedback from customers and potential customers with the help of short tailor-made surveys (Chapter 4 provides a few options on how to do that). Offer free or discounted product or service as an incentive. If you're a start up, don't spend big money you don't have on those surveys. As I mentioned previously, we learned that lesson the hard way at the *Pacific Coast Business Times.*

Alternatives to Sole Proprietorship

Not everyone sets up as the sole owner of his or her small business. Several other options can work if you approach them properly.

The franchise option

Aspiring entrepreneurs often look to franchising—owning and operating a business under an already-established brand. For some, in the right place at the right time with the right disposition, approach, and dreams, franchising can work, and work handsomely. For others, franchising might not be the answer. One aspect of franchising, however, is undisputed—its big and growing bigger role in the U.S. economy. The franchising sector of the U.S. economy expanded more than 18 percent from 2001 to 2005, adding more than 1.2 million jobs, and growing its direct economic output by more than 40 percent, from $624.6 billion to $880.9 billion, according to the International Franchise Association Educational Foundation.[1] Consider a few more numbers. Franchised businesses:

- Operated 909,253 establishments in the United States in 2005 (including those owned by franchisees and franchisors).

- Accounted for 3.3 percent of all business establishments in the United States.

- Provided 11 million jobs for a $278.6 billion payroll.

- Accounted for 8.1 percent of all private sector jobs, 5.3 percent of all private-sector payroll, and 4.4 percent of all private sector economic output.

Of course, much of this franchise success comes one small business at a time. Near-penniless-immigrant-turned-Domino's-Pizza-success-story Hishmeh offers his take on what works and what doesn't in the small-business franchise. "The big difference between running a franchise and running a privately named company," says Hishmeh, "is that in running a franchise you have to be willing to give up some of the freedom you have as an owner. For example, you have to follow a franchisor's operating rules."

"If you're a person who is very innovative and wants to do your own things, franchising is NOT for you," he adds. "If you also are someone who has to make your own procedures and policies, franchising also is NOT for you. But if you are willing to follow guidelines that are set by the franchisor, chances are you're going to be happy and successful because this model works."

The perfect partnership

There's nothing like going into business with your best friend, your most esteemed colleague, your favorite trusted advisor, or even your significant other. Just remember to get the terms of the deal in writing and up front. Spell out everything, down to division of property, debts, personal loans to the company, and responsibilities in the event of a breakup. "It's a premarital agreement, if you will," says SCORE's Lehman, "and should spell out 'who gets the children.' Have an attorney look at it, too," he adds. Lehman, a former partner in a small women's apparel chain, knows firsthand why that agreement is so important. He and his partner didn't have such an agreement, and they split acrimoniously. But, he adds, "Every day, hopefully we learn."

Tap Into Organizations

We've said it throughout this book, but it's definitely worth saying again: Plenty of professional, private, and government organizations are available with a wealth of information, help, and guidance for small businesses (see Addendum A for a listing of a few of them). Whether you're looking for industry benchmarks, funding options, alternative business models, help with organizational dynamics, a little advice from experts, a chat with your peers, or even potential employees, it's all available, some of it free, some low-cost, and some not so much. All you have to do is ask. That's often tough for us do-it-yourselfers. But to truly succeed long term, a small-business owner needs the wisdom to recognize his or her limitations, and the humility to ask for help.

"E" Business in Your Plans

As small-business owners, we must embrace the E, as in electronic, computer-aided management and business tools, and the Internet. E-based technologies can help grow our businesses and make our jobs easier, whether it's figuring payroll deductions, monitoring cash flow, tracking inventory, marketing to customers, selling our product, or even enabling virtual workplaces and spaces. "We've been able to grow our business without the addition of staff with the help of technology," says Garrett Planning Network's Garrett.

Of course, as with anything else, there's a right and wrong way to go about adopting and using technology, especially when it comes to selling products online.

The perfect equality

"The Web is the one environment where the small business can compete with its Big Box competition on a level playing field," says Meyerov, the successful entrepreneur and 12-year veteran Website designer.

"From what we have seen in more than a decade of dealing with small business in this space, there is only one product or service that is ever bought or sold on Internet. And that product or service is called credibility," says Meyerov. "If an end user does not feel that the small-business owner, the Website they are seeing, and the business that stands behind it is credible, they will not trust the company or hand over their hard-earned money to purchase. A Website should reflect an effective brand," add Meyerov.

"Unfortunately it's no better or worse in reality than if a potential customer walks into a very-high-end retail store and hands over his or her credit card details. The difference is that those customers know the store is there; they know they can see people, and they have a greater sense of credibility. With the online environment, it's very easy for the end user to simply click off a site and go to the next one on their search results."

There's no excuse for your business to come up short online. OnlyBusiness.com is hardly the only option on the online block. You can choose to work with an individual Web designer, or buy into the one-stop shops such as OnlyBusiness, GoDaddy.com, YahooStores, or MicrosoftLive, and more that provide cookie-cutter templates or individualized models to build your presence, or something else entirely.

But do keep in mind the importance of differentiating your product, your service, your brand. Do you want a "cookie-cutter" Website, or do you want to stand out from the pack?

Industry associations often can help direct you to various options. Also, network with fellow small businesses to find possible Web designer contractors. If you take that route, though, a few words of advice:

- Get references and check them out.
- Make sure your expectations are spelled out in writing.
- Get the cost structure spelled out in writing, too.
- Find out if the price includes ongoing Web hosting, and whether ongoing service is included, too.

Software and services to ease your job

If you're still using cumbersome paper journals for all your bookkeeping and recordkeeping, it's time to move on and admit, finally, that computers and the Internet are here to stay. Get moving and get connected. Without that connection, you're seriously handicapping your ability to compete successfully long term. Besides, computers do make your job easier in the long run—honest! Even the biggest holdouts become converts once they're comfortable with the technology.

Beyond computerizing your records and using off-the-shelf software to help track and control numbers and information, and to handle your customers, you may want to consider Web-based software known as SaaS (software as a service). This growing trend is an alternative—generally a lower-cost one—to purchasing software or a license to use it, installing it on your system, and then being responsible for maintenance, updates, and more. Instead, with SaaS, a company that owns the software, you can access it and work with it in an online environment for a small fee. Applications for this kind of service include payroll processing and other HR functions, Web content management, accounting, IT services, customer relationship management, and more. However, if you do choose this service, be sure that the delivery process doesn't adversely affect your customers or your employee.

Final Thoughts

"I don't think you can be an entrepreneur and not be ultra-optimistic," says Rogers. "Therefore it's easy to assume that if you just work hard enough and you're smart enough, you'll end up with the best-case scenario or at least something in the middle. Instead, you need to plan for the worst-case scenario while you're preparing for that best case," she adds.

Take off the rose-colored glasses and get ready to hunker down. Seek out the doomsday people, the devil's advocates, says CableOrganizer.com's Holstein. "Get their advice, because they will tell you what can go wrong."

Rogers offers another bit of hard-earned advice: "If you're going to start a business, don't have a recession—I've done that. We didn't go under, but we had competitors that went right over the edge."

What was Rogers's company's secret to survival? "Every single client was 100-percent happy with what we did for them, and I honestly think that's what made the difference. We always thought about the value of each client, and not the value of each product. Our goal was not to sell product, but to help our clients improve their businesses."

■ ■ ■ ■ ■ ■ ■

If your business simply tries to sell more stuff,
you'll end up competing on price. But if you try to help
improve your customers' lives, you will sell more stuff.
—Martha Rogers

■ ■ ■ ■ ■ ■ ■

Whatever you and your company are doing, persevere and keep doing it, adds Holstein.

Warren Buffett invented the concept of the time value of money, that if you put $100 a month every month in a bank account from the time you're a child, by the time you're an adult, you're a millionaire with the help of compounding interest. That doesn't just apply to putting money in the bank. As a kid out of college, if you start your own business and each year it grows, in ten years, you'll have a multimillion-dollar company. Don't get disheartened if you're making less money than your neighbor, just keep growing and improving it, and before you know it, you'll be huge.

■ ■ ■ ■ ■ ■ ■

As a small-business owner, success is not like a skyrocket.
At least for me it's been a steady crawl that comes with
hard work and staying focused.
—Cathey Finlon

■ ■ ■ ■ ■ ■

Vera Bradley's Miller offers her take on turning an idea into a successful business long term. "The beginning is the hardest because it's all about discovery and building your team," says Miller. "Once you've been in business for awhile, you have a team of people that, hopefully, can do things better than you can."

"[Co-founder and co-president] Barbara [Bradley Baekgaard] always says, 'It's like bringing a baby home from the hospital, and then years later that *baby* is six-foot-three and a young adult, and you think, 'How did it go from that infant to a six-three adult?' Well, you just do it day by day by day. You have to crawl before you walk, and walk before you run," says Miller. "I always thought, every day when I opened the door to come into work, it was a different company, and if it wasn't, we weren't doing the right thing because we weren't growing. When you grow you change. Everyday it *should* be different company as far as where you are and what you are doing, because if you're stagnant, you're not growing, and you have to grow, either in expertise or sales or whatever."

Your Ammunition

Some essentials to remember from this chapter include:

- Quality control is essential. Pay attention to it. Talk to your customers. They're your best source of whether you and your business are doing it right or not.

- Know your business, your product, your service, and your customers, and you vastly increase your chances for long-term success.

- If yours is a partnership, make sure you have a "pre- (or post-) marital" agreement that spells out in writing each partner's responsibilities, assets, and liabilities, as well as an orderly process in the event of dissolution of the partnership.

- Software and SaaS (software as a service) providers can make your job easier. But be sure to use both correctly. If you outsource, make sure to do so only if it enhances your customers' experience.

- The Internet can level the battlefield between you and the Big Box. Take advantage of that.

- If you don't know something or don't understand it, have the wisdom to recognize the fact, get educated, and seek out others who do understand what you don't.

ADDENDUM A

WHERE TO GO FOR MORE INFORMATION

Aberdeen Group (*www.aberdeen.com*): Aberdeen Group measures the benefits of technology in business, and makes the results comprehensible to the business world.

Administaff's HRTools.com (*www.hrtools.com*): "Toolkits" provide one-stop resources on personnel situations from hiring to firing and the safety, training, discipline, benefits, and legal compliance questions in between.

AllBusiness.com (*www.allbusiness.com*): Find practical advice for "real world questions" via how-to articles, business forms, blogs, business news, directories, product reviews and more. AllBusiness.com is a Dun & Bradstreet (*www.d&b.com*) company.

American Express OPEN (*https://home.americanexpress.com/ home/open.shtml*): Find information about the American Express OPEN card for businesses. Don't miss the Open Forum, a video and discussion forum for members.

Association of Small Business Development Centers (*www.asbdc-us.org*): Read articles, find a Small Business Development Center near you, or learn about SBDC services including free consulting and low-cost training for entrepreneurs.

Better Business Bureau (*www.bbb.org*): Browse a business library or find out how to make your business BBB-accredited. Be sure to check out BBBTips, a great source of information and direction from the BBB Consumer Education Foundation.

Biznik.com (*http://biznik.com*): A business-building social network for independent professionals and people building their own businesses, the site emphasizes collaboration, not competition.

Business Know-How (*www.businessknowhow.com*): Organized into sections such as Home Business, Start a Business, and Human Resources, this Website compiles hundreds of news articles, blogs, and tips. It is owned by Attard Communications, Inc., of Centerreach, New York.

Business Owner's Toolkit (*www.toolkit.com*): This free information and advice Website is from CCH Incorporated, a Wolters Kluwer business and a leading tax and legal information provider to professionals.

Capital One Financial Corporation (*www.capitalone.com*): Check the Resource tab under Small Business to find tools on topics including fraud, cyber-security, and company credit cards.

CBIZ/MHM (*www.cbiz.com*): CBIZ is a tech, accounting, wealth management, and HR services firm with 160 offices nationwide.

Center for Creative Leadership (*www.ccl.org*): The Center for Creative Leadership's research, education, and publications promote leadership on the individual and organizational levels. Find training online or through one of its domestic and international offices.

Disney Entrepreneur Center (*www.disneyec.com*): Founded in 2003 as a small business development organization for central Florida, Disney's E-Center also provides some resources through the Website.

Ewing Marion Kauffman Foundation: Find news and macro trends on entrepreneurship (*www.entrepreneurship.org*) or check out the resources for high-growth entrepreneurs with lots of useful articles, information, and direction on everything from operations to finance and HR, and more (*http://eventuring.kauffman.org*). These sites are part of the Ewing Marion Kauffman Foundation (*www.kauffman.org*), a foundation dedicated to supporting entrepreneurship and youth education.

Financial Planning Association (*www.fpanet.org*): General Public section features articles and planning tools for life goals and financial crises.

InsideCRM.com (*www.insidecrm.com*): Find news, free Webinars, event listings, a directory, product reviews, and other resources for sales and marketing professionals.

International Coach Federation (*www.coachfederation.org*): This international, independent, nonprofit group of personal and business coaches provides coaching credentials recognized worldwide. The Website caters to members, prospective members, and businesspeople seeking a coach.

ITBusinessEdge (*www.itbusinessedge.com*): This site offers plenty of useful tools and templates for, among other things, IT management. Check out its IT Manager's Toolkit.

John M. McKee (*www.businesssuccesscoach.net*): A successful author and business coach offers free leadership tips and information on his coaching and speaking services. Also see McKee's BusinessWomanWeb.com (*www.businesswomanweb.com*), with books for women in management positions and a useful Links page.

MasterCard Small Business (*www.mastercard.com/us/business/en/smallbiz/*): Articles and podcasts address self-employment, startups, women- and minority-owned businesses, and more. Midsized companies, corporations and the government and public sector have their own corners of the Website.

National Association of Women Business Owners (*www.nawbo.org*): This organization seeks to influence public policy and to promote economic development among women business owners. The Website offers articles, videos, and other resources, as well as encouraging strategic partnerships among its members.

National Dialogue on Entrepreneurship (*www.publicforuminstitute.org/nde/index.htm*): From the Public Forum Institute (*www.publicforuminstitute.org*), the site offers information, dialogue, and commentary on entrepreneurship, going beyond its role in job creation.

NFIB (*www.nfib.com*): From the grassroots activist National Federation of Independent Business, this site has all kinds of networking, information, trends, and lots more for small businesses.

OnlyBusiness.com (*www.onlybusiness.com*): A reasonably priced approach to designing, launching, and hosting a custom Website for your small business; prices range from $9.99 to $99.99 a month.

Onward Small Biz (*http://smallbiz.att.com*): AT&T's small business Website offers interactive courses, news, and tips on a variety of topics, including—but not at all limited to—the Web and wireless technology. Check out "The Watercooler," a chat forum for small business owners.

RightNowTechnologies (*www.rightnow.com*): This customer relationship management software solutions provider also offers helpful information in its Resources and Blog sections.

SCORE (*www.score.org*): The Service Corps of Retired Executives, a nonprofit organization associated with the U.S. Small Business Administration, has 389 chapters and 10,500 volunteers, including working and retired executives and business owners. Find out about free and confidential one-on-one counseling, or browse the online course material.

Small Business Administration (*www.sba.gov*): From the federal government, the site and its various sister sites offer all kinds of valuable information, advice, and direction on a vast catalog of topics.

Small Business Online Community from Bank of America (*http://smallbusinessonlinecommunity.bankofamerica.com/index.jspa*): You don't need to be a Bank of America customer to sign up for free services, such as participating in online events and peer forums, reading, and rating articles, sharing your story, and networking. Nonmembers can read articles and chats as well.

SmartBiz (*www.smartbiz.com*): The site offers Internet and technology resources for small business include articles, white papers, blogs, and product reviews.

Society of Human Resource Management (*www.shrm.org*): The largest professional HR management group, SHRM offers on its Website a thorough examination of human resource topics through articles, videos, Webcasts, books, and more.

U.S. Department of Labor (*www.dol.gov*): From the federal government, this site includes plenty of information on legal compliance for all kinds of labor laws, and even has downloadable versions of posters that must be posted in various workplaces.

ADDENDUM B

ELEMENTS OF A BUSINESS PLAN

Following are some essential elements that should be included in an effective business plan. Each should be thought out and in writing *before* a business gets off the ground. When putting together your own business plan, be sure to include specifics under each category, and honest in your projections:

- **Goal:** Explain your business and how you intend to achieve profitability.

- **Overview:** Show how your plan dovetails with financial goals and describe the market for your product/service. Can the market deliver the customer base you need to be profitable?

- **Risk factors:** Use bullet points to briefly spell out the potential pitfalls that may lie ahead in terms of competition, market risk, and your own experience and training gaps.

- **Management:** Describe who will manage the business and his or her qualifications. Be realistic and recognize that you can't and shouldn't be everything to your business.

- **Target audience:** Who are your potential customers? Support your assessment with facts and figures. If yours is a business-to-consumer operation, talk about which demographic groups can afford your product.

- **Economic outlook:** What's the current economic overview in your business sector? Is it growing or shrinking? Explain how your business can succeed within those limitations.

- **Capital structure:** Explain how you will balance debt and equity. Describe what kind of cash contribution the founder(s) will make. Outside investors like to see a commitment to business. Explain where you hope to get the rest of your capital and how the ownership will be structured.

- **Returns to investors:** How do you plan to reward investors and over what time frame?

- **Exit strategies:** Explain what your long term plans are. Will you plan to retain the business long-term, or sell it, and how will you achieve that goal? What's the long-term role of your investors?

- **Advertising/marketing strategies:** How do you plan to promote your business? List the details, and not just pipe dreams. Be realistic in your goals and projections. Include solid commitments/cost of the commitments.

- **Production/distribution:** How do you plan to produce/distribute your product or service? Be detailed and include costs and commitments required.

- **Staffing:** Lay out the personnel requirements for your business, and include costs for those staffers. Don't forget payroll preparation and benefits costs, turnover issues, and potential incentives.

■ **Competition:** Expand on the risk factors (above) to explain primary competitors for your product or service, and the potential for others to compete with you if you experience initial success. Explain your plan to differentiate your product/service from the rest of the pack.

■ **Logistics/technology:** Where do you plan to locate your business and why? What are the physical needs for the business and the costs? If it's business-to-consumer or even business-to-business, include issues such as access, parking, traffic, and more. What kind of equipment is needed and is it readily available? If not, how do you plan to acquire the equipment?

■ **Projected schedule of operations:** Include the various phases of operation with a time frame, tasks, and financial summary related to each.

NOTES

Chapter 1

1. U.S. Small Business Administration Office of Advocacy, "Frequently Asked Questions, Advocacy Small Business Statistics and Research," August 2007, How many small businesses are there? *http://app1.sba.gov/faqs/faqIndexAll.cfm?areaid=24* (accessed August 26, 2008).

2. U.S. Small Business Administration Office of Advocacy, "Private Firms, Establishments, Employment, Annual Payroll and Receipts by Firm Size, 1988-2005," Ann. Pay *http://www.sba.gov/advo/research/us88_05.pdf* (accessed August 28, 2008).

3. U.S. Small Business Administration Office of Advocacy, "Frequently Asked Questions, Advocacy Small Business Statistics and Research," August 2007, How important to economy;

what is small firm's share of employ, *http://
app1.sba.gov/faqs/faqIndexAll.cfm?areaid=24* (accessed
August 26, 2008).

4. U.S. Small Business Administration Office of Advocacy, "Frequently Asked Questions, Advocacy Small
Business Statistics and Research," August 2007,
chart/Starts and Closures, *http://app1.sba.gov/
faqs/faqIndexAll.cfm?areaid=24* (accessed August 26,
2008).

5. Bureau of Labor Statistics' Office of Employment and
Unemployment, "Survival and Longevity in the Busi-
ness Employment Dynamics," by Amy E. Knaup,
Monthly Labor Review, May 2005, Results, p. 51.
www.bls.gov/opub/mlr/2005/05/ressum.pdf (accessed
August 27, 2008).

6. U.S. Bankruptcy Courts, "Business and Nonbusi-
ness Bankruptcy Cases Commenced, By Chapter of
the Bankruptcy Code, during the 12-Month Period
Ended September 30, 2007," Table F-2,
www.uscourts.gov/bnkrpctystats/sept2007/f2table.xls (accessed July 15, 2008).

7. U.S. Bankruptcy Courts, "Business and Nonbusi-
ness Bankruptcy Cases Commenced, By Chapter of
the Bankruptcy Code, during the 12-Month Period
Ended September 30, 2006," Table F-2;
*www.uscourts.gov/bnkrpctystats/sept2006/
f2table_jun2006.xls* (accessed July 15, 2008)

8. U.S. Small Business Administration, Business Bankruptcy Project, "Financial Difficulties of Small Businesses and Reasons for their Failure," SBA-95-0403,
by Teresa A. Sullivan, Elizabeth Warren, and Jay
Westbrook, September 1998, Executive Summary,
pp. 3–4; *www.sba.gov/advo/research/rs188tot.pdf* (accessed August 27, 2008).

9. Pew Internet and American Life Project, "Online Shopping: Convenient but Risky," by John B. Horrigan, Associate Director, Pew Internet and American Life Project, Pew Research Center Publications, *http://pewresearch.org/pubs/733/online-shopping* (accessed August 28, 2008).

10. NFIB, 411 Small Business Facts, *Competition, 2003, www.411sbfacts.com/sbpoll.php?POLLID=0012& KT_back=1* (accessed August 10, 2008).

Chapter 2

1. Kauffman Index of Entrepreneurial Activity, Ewing Marion Kauffman Foundation, "Entrepreneurship;" (© 2008 Ewing Marion Kauffman Foundation; *www.kauffman.org) www.kauffman.org/items.cfm?itemID=1036* (accessed August 27, 2008).

2. American Express OPEN Small Business Monitor, April 21, 2008, "Focus on Growth and Hiring Plans Remain as Optimism in the Economy Drops for Small Business Owners," *http://home3.americanexpress.com/corp/pc/2008/sbmonitor.asp* (accessed August 28, 2008).

3. American Express® OPEN Small Business Monitor, May 24, 2007, "Small Business Optimism is on an Upswing" *http://home3.americanexpress.com/corp/pc/2007/monitor.asp* (accessed August 28, 2008).

4. U.S. Small Business Administration, "Small Business Assessment Readiness Tool," *http://app1.sba.gov/sbat/index.cfm?Tool=4* (accessed August 28, 2008).

Chapter 3

1. Society of Human Resource Management, "2007 Job Satisfaction: A Survey Report by the Society for Human Resource Management," June 2007, p. 16, Fig. 1 "A Comparison of 'Very Important' Aspects of Employee Job Satisfaction."

2. Society of Human Resource Management, "2007 Job Satisfaction: A Survey Report by the Society for Human Resource Management," June 2007, p. 12, Fig. 1 *Very Important Aspects of Employee Job Satisfaction.*"

3. NFIB, 411 Small Business Facts, *Innovation,* Volume 5, Issue 6, 2005, *www.411sbfacts.com/sbpoll.php?POLLID=0046&KT_back=1* (accessed August 27, 2008).

4. Magos, Alice, Ask Alice Online Advice Columnist, Business Owner's Toolkit, "Ask Alice About Recruiting and Retaining Employees," *www.toolkit.com/news/newsDetail.aspx?aa=1&nid=07-226askalice* (accessed August 27, 2008).

5. PaulOrfalea.com, "Paul Orfalea Biography," *www.paulorfalea.com/profile.html* (accessed August 28, 2008).

6. Better Business Bureau, "Ways to Keep Your Employees Happier," 2002, *www.bbb.org/alerts/article.asp?ID=397* (accessed August 28, 2008).

7. Administaff, "Administaff Announces Results of Business Confidence Survey," August 13, 2008, *http://phx.corporate-ir.net/phoenix.zhtml?c=105568&p=irol-newsArticle&ID=1144000&highlight* (accessed August 28, 2008).

8. ITAC, The Telework Advisory Group for WorldatWork, "*Telework Trending Upward,*" February 8, 2007. © 2008. Reprinted with permission from WorldatWork. Content is licensed for use by purchaser only. No part of this article may be reproduced, excerpted, or redistributed in any form without express written permission from WorldatWork.

9. CDW, "2008 CDW Telework Report Reveals One Foot on the Gas, One Foot on the Brake," *http://newsroom.cdw.com/news-releases/news-release-03-31-08.html* (accessed August 27, 2008).

10. SurePayroll, "SurePayroll Insights Survey: Business Owners Share Opinions and Advice on Firing People," March 16, 2007, w*ww.surepayroll.com/spsite/press/releases/2007/release031607.asp* (accessed August 28, 2008).

11. U.S. Department of Labor, "Workplace Poster Requirements for Small Businesses and Other Employers," *www.dol.gov/PrinterFriendly/PrinterVersion.aspx?url=www.dol.gov/osbp/sbrefa/poster/matrix.htm* (accessed August 28, 2008).

Chapter 4

1. NFIB, 411 Small Business Facts, "Marketing Perspectives," Volume 6, Issue 8, 2006, *www.411sbfacts.com/sbpoll.php?POLLID=0054&KT_back=1* (accessed August 27, 2008).

2. American Express OPEN Small Business Monitor, October 1, 2007, "Small Business Owners Hold the Line...," Small Business Owners Plan to Invest in Technology and Marketing, *http://home3.americanexpress.com/corp/pc/2007/07sbm.asp* (accessed August 28, 2008).

Chapter 5

1. Hultman, Claes, and Gerald E. Hills, "Marketing Perspectives," 6 (2006): 6. *www.nfib.com/object/sbPolls* (accessed August 28, 2008).

2. Mackay, Harvey. *www.harveymackay.com/pdfs/mackay66.pdf* (accessed August 12, 2008)

Chapter 7

1. "Focus on Growth and Hiring Plans Remain as Optimism in the Economy Drops for Small Business Owners," American Express OPEN Small Business Monitor, April 21, 2008, *http://home3.americanexpress.com/corp/pc/2008/sbmonitor.asp* (accessed August 28, 2008).

2. "411 Small Business Facts," *Advice and Advisors*, NFIB, 2 (2002), *www.411sbfacts.com/ sbpoll.php?POLLID=0012&KT_back=1* (accessed August 28, 2008).

Chapter 8

1. "Economic Impact of Franchised Businesses, Volume 2," *International Franchise Association, Executive Summary and Highlights*, March 12, 2008, *www.franchise.org/uploadedFiles/Franchisors/ Other_Content/economic_impact_documents/ EconImpact_Vol2_HiLights.pdf* (accessed August 28, 2008).

INDEX

ABOUT THE AUTHORS

Coauthors Henry Dubroff and Susan J. Marks are ideally suited to help entrepreneurs and small-business owners understand what it takes and learn how to develop long-term success for their businesses. Both are well-known financial journalists and entrepreneurs, and together they have developed and produced award-winning projects.

Dubroff is founder, owner, and editor of the *Pacific Coast Business Times*, a company that grew from a business plan on paper into a highly successful business journal serving the Santa Barbara–Ventura–San Luis Obispo area of California's coast. Despite operating in the shadow of the region's Big Boxes—read that "deep pockets"—competition in the Los Angeles media market, Dubroff's small business reached break-even only 18 months after launch and continues to maintain double-digit growth rates.

Dubroff and his entrepreneurial accomplishments have been recognized by the U.S. Chamber of Commerce, the U.S. Small Business Administration, Ernst & Young through its Entrepreneur of the Year Awards, and the California Legislature.

Marks is an award-winning journalist, freelance writer, and book author and editor specializing in consumer issues. She has collaborated on or written a dozen successful business and personal-finance self-help and motivational books. She's also written articles for a variety of publications on topics ranging from small business and technology to e-commerce, personal finance, workplace, careers, and healthcare.

In her nearly 30 years of newspaper, magazine, and book writing and editing experience, Marks has chronicled large- and small-business successes and failures, innovations and changes, and has helped all kinds of people all over the world deliver their messages and tell their stories in ways that all of us can easily understand. Her work has received awards and recognition from local, regional, and national professional and industry organizations.